LEGO® STAR WARS™

CHOOSE YOUR PATH

WRITTEN BY **SIMON HUGO**

WELCOME TO YOUR GALACTIC ADVENTURE!

In this book, **you** are in charge of where to go! Pick one of the three starting points opposite and journey through the LEGO® Star Wars™ galaxy. Meet your favorite characters and creatures, jump into awesome vehicles, and travel from planet to planet.

On every page, you will discover lots of incredible LEGO Star Wars facts. Then you will face two options for where to go next. Some options will lead to endings—some endings are better than others!

Once you reach an ending, where will you go next? Will you retrace your steps or pick a new starting point for a whole new adventure?

I'M READY FOR ADVENTURES—LET'S GO!

YOUR PERSONAL GUIDE

Protocol droid U-3PO is here to accompany you on your adventures and give you advice. Look out for him on the pages of this book, but watch out! His suggestions might not always be helpful!

WHERE WILL YOU GO FIRST?

HUNT THE SITH

The galaxy is in chaos! A menacing group called the Separatists is attacking planets. There are rumors that the ancient villains known as the Sith have returned. Help Jedi Obi-Wan Kenobi track down the Sith. Can you protect the galaxy from the dark side of the Force?

OR

FIGHT THE EMPIRE

The evil Sith Lord Darth Sidious has made himself the Emperor of the galaxy. The Rebel Alliance has come together to fight against his Empire. Join Princess Leia and the Rebel Alliance in their fight to restore peace to the galaxy. Do you have what it takes to defeat the Empire?

OR

DEFEAT THE FIRST ORDER

The galaxy faces a new threat. The dangerous First Order want to take control. Help scavenger Rey and her friends escape from its clutches aboard the *Millennium Falcon*. Can you stop the First Order before it is too late?

TURN 1

TURN 2

TURN 3

JEDI STARFIGHTER ADVENTURE

di Obi-Wan Kenobi has
nsed the presence of an
il Sith Lord somewhere
the galaxy. Obi-Wan takes
in his Jedi ship, which
nnects to a hyperdrive
g to make it travel at
htspeed. Jump into your
n ship and join him.
here will you go first?

DATA FILE

**DELTA-7 JEDI
INTERCEPTOR**

» Travels at lightspeed
  when boosted by
  hyperspace ring

» 2 laser cannons

» Astromech droid
  socket

Obi-Wan Kenobi
in cockpit

There are signs of Sith activity
on the planet Tatooine. Head
there first.

TURN TO
13

OR

Join the clone troopers on the
planet Utapau to find out what
they know.

TURN TO
9

BIG, ROUND BOOSTER

A hyperdrive ring gives an
extra boost to a starfighter's
engines during long-distance
travel. The ship detaches from
the ring after lightspeed travel,
to land or go into battle.

When Princess Leia picks you for a secret rebel mission, you jump at the chance to fight the evil Empire that rules the galaxy. But when her ship comes under attack from Imperial stormtroopers while you are aboard, you start to feel a little less bold! The *Tantive IV* is not heavily armed, so you can't beat them in battle. What can you do instead?

DATA FILE

CR90 CORVETTE

» Top speed 950 kph (590 mph)

» 4 laser cannons

» 2 twin turbolasers

» 8 small and 4 large laser-armed escape pods

SECRET REBEL SHIP

The *Tantive IV* is officially a diplomatic ship in the service of Princess Leia's home planet, Alderaan. Leia and her adoptive father, Bail Organa, use its official status as a cover for secret rebel missions against the Empire.

You let the stormtroopers capture you and take you aboard their ship. Maybe you can bring down the enemy from within!

TURN TO
4

OR

Make your getaway in an escape pod and blast off into the unknown. Anywhere's better than staying with the stormtroopers!

TURN TO
7

MILLENNIUM FALCON UNDER FIRE

Danger! The *Millennium Falcon* is under attack! You and your droid, U-3PO, are aboard when it comes under fire from the evil First Order, which is out to control the galaxy and clamp down on rebellion. The ship's rebel pilots, Rey and Chewbacca, want to escape by dodging the enemy fire. But U-3PO thinks you should make a hasty but dangerous jump to lightspeed. What do you do?

DATA FILE

CORELLIAN YT-1300F LIGHT FREIGHTER

» Top speed 1,050 kph (650 mph)

» 2 quad lasers and 1 blaster cannon

» Made the Kessel Run in less than 12 parsecs

NOT-SO-CAREFUL OWNERS

The *Millennium Falcon* is one of the fastest ships in the galaxy. It used to belong to the smuggler and rebel hero Han Solo. He won it from a friend in a card game, but it was stolen years later. Rey rescued it from a junkyard on Jakku.

You go with Rey's suggestion and try to dodge the First Order fire above the planet Jakku.

TURN TO 11

OR

You listen to U-3PO and choose to get as far away as possible by jumping to lightspeed.

TURN TO 25

PRISONER OF THE EMPIRE

Now a prisoner of the Empire, you are taken from the *Tantive IV* onto an enormous Star Destroyer. Inside, you are marched toward a holding cell. As you go, you pass hundreds of stormtroopers and vast launch bays full of TIE fighter attack ships. You realize this is much scarier than you thought... this ship acts as a mobile base for the Empire! Can you risk making a run for it or should you bide your time?

DATA FILE

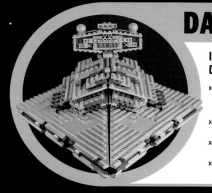

IMPERIAL STAR DESTROYER

» Top speed 975 kph (606 mph)

» 68 heavy turbolasers

» 60 ion cannons

» 8 turret gun stations

DEADLY DESTROYERS

Star Destroyers are the Empire's biggest battleships. They can deploy a fleet of TIE fighters in just a few seconds, and are used to spread fear and crush rebellion across the galaxy.

Carry on to the holding cell. There are too many Imperial forces around for you to risk taking them on!

TURN TO **15**

OR

Make a break for one of the launch bays and try to find an unguarded TIE fighter to take off in.

TURN TO **10**

When you reach the rebel fleet, you dock with *Home One*, its biggest and most important ship. Once aboard, you meet the leaders of the Rebel Alliance, who want to defeat the Empire once and for all. Your task is to shut down a vital Imperial power station. What ship will you choose for this mission?

LEADERS' SHIP

Home One is the base for the rebel leadership. Its members include Mon Calamari soldier Admiral Ackbar, Imperial defector Crix Madine, reformed smuggler Lando Calrissian, and brave and noble politician Mon Mothma.

Mon Mothma

Admiral Ackbar

General Madine

General Calrissian

Speed is your best option. Select a small, fast rebel starfighter to blast your way to the power station!

TURN TO **43**

OR

Disguise is a much better idea. Choose a stolen Imperial shuttle to sneak past the Empire's defenses.

TURN TO **28**

BUILD IT!

Home One is huge, but your own base doesn't have to be. Make a tiny version that can fit in the palm of your hand.

Sending a distress call was risky since it could have been intercepted by the First Order! Luckily, the first ship to come to your aid is a Resistance Bomber—and it is enough to deter Kylo Ren, for now... This heavy bomber is on a secret mission for the Resistance. There is space inside for many important rebels. Would you like to join them?

DATA FILE

B/SF-17 HEAVY BOMBER

» 2 rear gun turrets

» Bomb deployment bay

» Carries key Resistance figures such as Vice Admiral Holdo

BOMBS AWAY!

The Resistance Bomber is designed to drop a heavy payload of proton explosives. It is crewed by a pilot, a bombardier, and two gunners, who defend the ship from rotating laser cannon turrets.

Don't go aboard, stay in the *Falcon* but follow the Resistance Bomber on its mission to the planet Crait.

TURN TO **114**

OR

You are keen to meet some of the key members of the Resistance so you leave the *Falcon* and board the bomber.

TURN TO **82**

Aboard the *Tantive IV*, you squeeze into an escape pod with U-3PO and two other droids: C-3PO and R2-D2. Escape pods are a spaceship's lifeboats. As soon as the door of your round pod is sealed, it blasts away, heading for the desert planet Tatooine. The pod lands with a thud and you step out to see nothing but sand in all directions. What should you do?

DATA FILE

CLASS-6 ESCAPE POD
» 4 escape thrusters
» 6 directional thrusters
» Room for 6 occupants

THE ODD COUPLE

C-3PO is a protocol droid. He doesn't really like excitement and would much rather be helping people to communicate in peace. R2-D2 is an astromech droid used to flying with fighter pilots, and is always ready for a new adventure!

C-3PO

Follow R2-D2 as he heads out in search of civilization on Tatooine.

TURN TO **12**

OR

Like C-3PO, you prefer to be cautious. Stay in the escape pod and wait to be rescued.

TURN TO **23**

THESE SAND DUNES ALL LOOK THE SAME! WE'LL GET LOST!

R2-D2

As you leave Niima Outpost and Unkar Plutt behind, you stumble across an abandoned quadjumper. Though unreliable, these ships are powerful and capable of space travel. This could be just the thing to get you out of here. However, as you start it up, its engines can be heard for miles around—attracting the attention of a First Order ship!

DATA FILE

QUADRIJET TRANSFER SPACETUG

» 4 large thrusters

» Magnetic cargo clamps

» Tractor beam projectors

FREIGHT SHIP

Quadjumpers are designed to move bulky cargo around space freight yards, but their powerful engines and small size also make them popular with crooks. Many smugglers upgrade them with weapons and hyperdrive systems.

TALK ABOUT GOING OUT WITH A BANG!

FALSE START!

Before you are off the ground, the First Order begins to fire at your ship! You and U-3PO only just jump clear before it explodes. As stormtroopers arrive to take you prisoner, you wish you had accepted Unkar's deal instead!

» GO BACK AND CHOOSE ANOTHER PATH!

ATTACK ON UTAPAU

When you arrive on the rocky planet of Utapau, you meet a squad of clone troopers. Suddenly, a tri-droid arrives and starts attacking. Your trusty companion, U-3PO, informs you that these deadly droids are commanded by General Grievous, a villainous cyborg who is in league with the Sith. Grievous could be close by! What do you do next?

BUILD IT!

A tri-droid has three legs. Try making a quad-droid, with four legs, or a uni-droid, with just one! Keep it stable so it stands up.

THREE-LEGGED DROID

The Octuptarra combat tri-droid is a tall, three-legged battle droid used by the menacing Separatists who are attacking the galaxy. It scuttles like a spider across Utapau's stony ground, firing its spinning laser cannons!

Laser cannon

I'D MUCH RATHER BE IN A RELAXING HOT OIL BATH!

Destroy the tri-droid and go with the clone troopers to search for Grievous. It's better to work as a team.

TURN TO **31**

OR

Leave the clone troopers to fight the tri-droid and go after Grievous alone. You can handle Grievous by yourself!

TURN TO **36**

TIE FIGHTER FLIGHT

You sprint away from your captors and leap into one of the TIE fighters. The hangar is full of docked TIEs so there are plenty to choose from. As U-3PO squeezes in too, you grab the controls and speed out of the Star Destroyer. You are far away when a message comes through from another Imperial ship. How should you respond?

DATA FILE

TWIN ION ENGINE SPACE SUPERIORITY STARFIGHTER

» Top speed 1,200 kph (746 mph)

» 2 laser cannons

» Wings have solar energy collectors

A SWARM OF TIES

TIE fighters are small and simple fighter craft, designed to be disposable. What they lack in weaponry they make up for in numbers—attacking in swarms and overwhelming their opponents in seemingly endless waves.

Ignoring the message might make the Imperials suspicious. You reply, pretending to be a fellow Imperial pilot.

TURN TO **74**

OR

You fear the other ship will recognize you for who you truly are, so you opt to outrun them instead.

TURN TO **60**

DESERT DUNES GETAWAY

Well done! You dodged the enemy fire and landed on the desert planet Jakku. Scavengers and First Order forces alike roam this world. The First Order is scanning the area in search of your ship, so you and Rey jump onto speeders to go in search of help. On your way to the nearest town, you see another speeder in the distance. Should you make contact or keep clear?

I'VE GOT SAND IN MY JOINTS— GET US OUT OF HERE FAST!

Rey

REY'S RIDE

Rey built her speeder out of parts she found and traded when she lived as a scavenger on Jakku. It is a one-of-a-kind craft, capable of hauling heavy loads or moving very fast without cargo.

DATA FILE

CUSTOM-BUILT SPEEDER

» Top speed 420 kph (260 mph)

» Engines from an old cargo ship

» Repulsorlifts from crashed X-wings

You carry on as planned to the nearest town, Niima Outpost, where you plan to ask Jakku locals for assistance.

TURN TO **24**

OR

The speeder you have spotted is closer than the town! Chase after it to ask for help.

TURN TO **38**

BUILD IT!

Make your own customized speeder by choosing parts that look like they have come from other vehicles. Rey's speeder is dark red. What color will yours be?

You cross the Tatooine desert until you get to a small farm. This is where Luke Skywalker lives with his Uncle Owen. Owen often deals with Jawa traders, who scavenge and sell spare vehicle and droid parts. When the Jawas see your group, they offer to take you on to the nearest spaceport, but Luke is keen to show off his flying skills first. Can you spare the time?

SECRET HISTORY

Luke Skywalker is the son of a brave and powerful Jedi Knight. But Uncle Owen doesn't want Luke following in such dangerous footsteps, so he has kept Luke's true family history a secret from him.

Treadwell droid

THESE JAWAS ARE LOOKING AT ME FUNNY...

Luke Skywalker

Uncle Owen

Jawa

Thank Luke for the offer, but there's no time! Head off with the Jawas to their sandcrawler.

TURN TO **64**

OR

Luke's vehicle is a T-16 skyhopper. You've never seen one in action! You make time to check it out.

TURN TO **52**

BUILD IT!

Most LEGO® droids are made from just a few parts. Scavenge a handful of bricks from your collection and create your own droid.

A DAY AT THE RACES

FORCE FACT!

The Sith work in pairs. There is only ever one master and one apprentice. They believe that by only having two Sith, they are harder to detect.

You arrive on Tatooine. Criminals and untrustworthy traders pull the strings on this dusty desert world, and they meet to make deals at podraces. You go to a race, looking for information, and get talking to some crooks in the crowd. They speak in hushed tones about the mighty Sith warrior that recently visited Tatooine, but they cannot agree on where he went next. Who can you believe?

RISKY RACERS

Podracing is a very dangerous but very popular sport. Competitors fly around a desert course in tiny cockpits pulled by enormous engines. Known as podracers, these craft are very fast, but not at all safe!

I DON'T TRUST ANY OF THESE CROOKS!

Some junk dealers tell you the Sith warrior went to cause trouble on the peaceful world of Naboo. Head there—fast!

TURN TO **44**

OR

Others have heard that the Sith went to Coruscant to meet with his master. You decide to go to the city planet to track him down.

TURN TO **30**

HOTH HIDEOUT

A journey through hyperspace brings you to the planet Hoth. This icy world is home to a rebel base hidden beneath the snow. As you explore the base and make new friends, you hear an alarm sound. Your new pal Luke Skywalker has gone missing in a snowstorm! How can you help find him?

ECHO LOCATION

The rebel outpost on Hoth is known as Echo Base. It is a mix of natural caves and spaces the rebels have carved out of the ice. The only clues to its location are the defensive cannons that surround it.

K-3PO

R3-A2

Princess Leia

Rebel troopers

Rebel officer

BRRR! DROIDS NEED COATS, TOO!

You wrap up warmly and follow a faint set of footprints in the snow —they could be Luke's!

TURN TO
77

OR

Head the other way. The footprints could belong to a wild animal. Luke would have stayed clear!

TURN TO
104

BUILD IT!

You can make your own LEGO footprint by putting a baseplate on the floor and building around the shape of your foot!

BOUNTY HUNTERS BREAK OUT!

In the Star Destroyer's holding cell you meet four bounty hunters. U-3PO recognizes them as Dengar, a hard-bitten human, Bossk, a ruthless Trandoshan, and 4-LOM and IG-88, two emotionless droids. Bounty hunters work for themselves and are notoriously untrustworthy. But together, they are planning a jailbreak. Will you join them?

WHO'S HUNTING WHOM?

Bounty hunters are tough and heartless trackers. If the price is right, they will work for anyone—trapping wanted individuals and delivering them into the hands of their enemies!

IG-88

Dengar

Bossk

4-LOM

I'VE GOT A BAD FEELING ABOUT THESE BOUNTY HUNTERS!

Help the four bounty hunters break out of the cell and go with them to their ship.

TURN TO **33**

OR

Join in the jailbreak, but sneak away from the others as soon as you are free.

TURN TO **19**

BUILD IT!

Build a cell for the bounty hunters, including prison bars, but add a collapsing wall for their breakout!

You brave your way through the sandstorm until you reach the crash site. There you find a First Order TIE fighter! These single-pilot vehicles are frequently seen on First Order worlds. For a crashed ship, it looks in very good condition, meaning top-quality parts for Plutt. As you move closer, U-3PO calls out a warning. He's seen a pilot moving inside!

DATA FILE

TIE/SF SPACE SUPERIORITY FIGHTER

» 2 laser cannons

» Missile launcher

» Reserved for elite Special Forces pilots

SUPER SPEED

Unlike most TIE fighters, the First Order's Special Forces TIE is equipped with a hyperdrive for lightspeed travel. This makes it suitable for long-range missions as well as hit-and-run attacks.

FOOLED BY PLUTT

Before you can react to U-3PO's warning, the TIE fighter lifts off the ground and aims its laser cannons at you. The ship isn't damaged at all and Unkar Plutt has sent you straight into a First Order trap!

» GO BACK AND CHOOSE ANOTHER PATH!

JABBA'S SAIL BARGE

When you ask to leave, Jabba says you are free to go—straight into the Great Pit of Carkoon! All those who displease Jabba are thrown into this massive pit. Whatever it contains can't be good. Jabba's sail barge flies you across the desert, where he orders you to walk the plank. Do you dare jump?

PARTY BARGE

Jabba likes to party on his barge as it skims above the sands of Tatooine. Food and drinks are served by droids, while music is played by the bright blue band leader Max Rebo.

Jabba's henchman Ree-Yees

R2-D2

Weequay guard

Band leader Max Rebo

Jabba

You might as well get it over with quickly! Take a deep breath and... jump!

TURN TO 91

OR

It's a long shot, but you try pleading for Jabba's mercy as you teeter on the edge.

TURN TO 100

DATA FILE

KHETANNA

» Jabba's sail barge
» Top speed 100 kph (62 mph)
» Sunshade sails
» Blaster cannon

You score a direct hit on Kylo Ren's weapons, leaving him no choice but to race back to his ship—a huge First Order Star Destroyer! The massive ship locks its tractor beam onto the *Falcon* and draws it aboard. You and U-3PO manage to climb out of the *Falcon* before the First Order stormtroopers reach your hangar. It's time to run, but where to?

FORCE FACT!
-- --- --
This ship houses a secret chamber for Supreme Leader Snoke—the sinister and shadowy First Order leader who is strong in the dark side of the Force!

NEW AND IMPROVED

The First Order Star Destroyers are more powerful and almost twice as long as their predecessors, which were the flagships of the old Empire. The colossal First Order ships can launch squadrons of TIE fighters in seconds.

DATA FILE

RESURGENT-CLASS BATTLECRUISER
» 1,500 turbolasers and ion cannons
» Carries more than 8,000 stormtroopers

U-3PO thinks he could hack the ship's computer so you go in search of the communications system.

TURN TO
41

OR

Hoping to find an escape vessel, you and U-3PO make your way to the Star Destroyer's cargo hold.

TURN TO
63

THAT'S NO MOON!

Now alone and free on the Star Destroyer, you and U-3PO look out a viewport and see a small moon. For a moment, you worry that you will crash into it. Then you realize it's no moon; it's the Empire's newest weapon, the Death Star—and your ship is docking with it! You sneak aboard the enormous battle station. Where should you go first?

BUILD IT!

You can use square bricks to build round shapes! Try to build a small Death Star without using curved pieces.

Governor Tarkin with Darth Vader

Superlaser

MEGA STAR

The Death Star is the biggest battle station the galaxy has ever seen. It is run by Grand Moff Wilhuff Tarkin—a cruel man willing to destroy whole planets!

You decide to try your luck at the prison level. You may be able to find others who will help you like on the Star Destroyer!

TURN TO 35

OR

Head for the control room and try to sabotage the Death Star before it causes real damage.

TURN TO 76

DATA FILE

THE DEATH STAR
» 7,000 TIE fighters on board
» 15,000 turbolasers
» One planet-destroying superlaser!
» 300,000+ crew

When you get to the Resistance-controlled planet of Crait, you see no sign of the Resistance Bombers you were searching for—only the scary sight of several First Order gorilla walkers! The side hatches of these massive machines open to reveal hordes of stormtroopers ready for action. Your situation has just gone from bad to worse!

DATA FILE

ALL TERRAIN MEGACALIBER SIX (AT-M6)

» Also known as the heavy assault walker or the gorilla walker

» At least 4 blaster cannons

BIG BEAST

Much bigger than the similar-looking AT-ATs once used by the Empire, the AT-M6 gets its name from the MegaCaliber Six cannon on its back. Its "gorilla walker" nickname comes from its powerful primate shape.

CRAIT CRASHDOWN

Swerving to avoid the fire from the assault walkers, the *Falcon* crashes down onto Crait. As the walkers and stormtroopers advance on your position, you can only wish you'd never become separated from the bombers in the first place!

>> GO BACK AND CHOOSE ANOTHER PATH!

RUNNER VS. WALKER

You know you can't beat the AT-ST, but you are determined to do it some damage before it blasts you! From the raised cockpit, the driver can survey the land and fire twin blasters. You prepare for the worst, but when its top hatch opens out pops a familiar, furry face. Instead of an Imperial pilot, you see your brave Wookiee pal, Chewbacca!

DATA FILE

ALL TERRAIN SCOUT TRANSPORT

» Top speed 90 kph (56 mph)

» 3 blaster cannons

» Used on Jedha, Hoth, and Endor

PLAYING CHICKEN

Stalking its prey on long, powerful legs, the All Terrain Scout Transport (AT-ST) goes where other vehicles cannot. Its unusual design does make its movements a little comical though, earning it the nickname "chicken walker"!

SHIELDS DOWN!

Chewie has stolen this walker and come to help you on your mission! You climb in with him, and together you blast the power station. Now the Death Star has no shields, and the rebels can end the Empire's rule. Good work!

>> GO BACK AND CHOOSE ANOTHER PATH!

BATTLE OF KASHYYYK

You arrive on Kashyyyk, the jungle homeworld of the Wookiees. The strong, hairy Wookiees used to live in peace, but there is nothing peaceful about their planet since the Separatists invaded! A band of Wookiees is bravely fighting battle droids and a towering Separatist spider droid. Will you stop to help them?

WALKING WEAPON

The OG-9 homing spider droid has a large laser cannon on top for attack and another one underneath for defense. Since it's a droid, it does not need a pilot.

Homing spider droid

Dwarf spider droid

You stay to fight alongside the Wookiees—they could use your help! Your search for the Sith Lord will have to wait.

TURN TO 47

OR

You can't waste time in your search for the Sith! You and Obi-Wan leave the Wookiees to fight their battle and race on.

TURN TO 71

BUILD IT!

Build a forest base where the Wookiees can hide from the Separatists. Use green and brown bricks and special tree pieces so that the base is well hidden!

TUSKEN TERROR

You take C-3PO's advice and stay with the escape pod. Together, you wait for a rescue team, and soon see some figures approaching. But these are not rescuers—they are Tusken Raiders, armed with clubs and sticks! As they prepare to attack, you look to the horizon for help. There are signs of life to the left and right. Which way will you run?

BUILD IT!

Tusken Raiders travel on big, hairy beasts called banthas. Why not build one for your Raiders to ride on?

RUNNING ON SAND IS REALLY HARD WORK, YOU KNOW.

Race right, where you see somebody riding on an animal.

TURN TO **37**

OR

Run left, where you spy a landspeeder crossing the desert.

TURN TO **42**

WATER WARRIORS

Tusken Raiders are the most dangerous natives on Tatooine. They are fiercely protective of every drop of water in the desert, and fear that outsiders will steal it. As a result, they tend to attack all newcomers!

UNKAR'S DEAL

Arriving at Niima Outpost, you meet the greedy trader Unkar Plutt. This thug controls the nearby junkyards and will buy anything if the price is right—from vehicles, weapons, and droids to spare parts, junk, and even information. Plutt says he will tell the First Order that the *Falcon* has already left Jakku if you bring him the parts from a TIE fighter that has crashed in the desert. Can he be trusted?

POWERFUL PLUTT

Unkar Plutt is a big deal on Jakku. When Rey lived on the planet, she had to give him all the salvage she could find in exchange for a tiny allowance of food.

Unkar Plutt

Rey

NO, THERE ARE NO DROIDS FOR SALE HERE!

You accept Unkar's deal and set off to look for the crashed TIE that he has demanded in return for your protection.

TURN TO **34**

OR

You don't trust Unkar to keep his word. Instead, you head off on your own to find another way out of your tight spot.

TURN TO **8**

BUILD IT!

Build some salvaged vehicle parts for Unkar to sell at Niima Outpost. Then combine them to make a spaceship out of mixed-up spare parts!

RUN-IN WITH REN

The *Falcon* jumps to lightspeed, taking you far away from Jakku. When you emerge from hyperspace, the first thing you see is a unique First Order TIE fighter with thin, angled wings approaching. U-3PO spots that this is no ordinary TIE. It's the personal attack ship of First Order commander Kylo Ren! How should you respond?

DATA FILE

TIE/VN SPACE SUPERIORITY FIGHTER

» Also known as the TIE Silencer

» Laser cannons

» Missile launchers

FORCE FOR EVIL

Kylo Ren is a powerful Force user who wants to destroy the Jedi and their peaceful ideals. As a leader in the First Order, he commands the armies and warships to make his wish come true! This TIE fighter is his latest vehicle.

You don't think you can outrun Kylo Ren so you use the *Falcon's* laser cannon to target Kylo Ren's weapons.

TURN TO **18**

OR

You take aim to fight, but don't think you will succeed without backup, so you send out a distress call as well.

TURN TO **6**

TIE ADVANCED

You struggle to keep up with the mystery ship in the T-16, but you do get close enough to see it properly. U-3PO says it is a TIE Advanced—one of the Empire's most dangerous starfighters. He has heard of just one individual who flies a ship like it, and that is Darth Vader himself!

DATA FILE

TWIN ION ENGINE ADVANCED X1

» Top speed 1,200 kph (746 mph)

» 2 laser cannons

» Cluster missile launcher

IMPERIAL ENFORCER

Part man, part machine, the villainous Darth Vader is the Empire's chief enforcer. His job is to crush rebellion wherever he finds it. He is a brilliant pilot and almost unstoppable in combat. He flies this specially modified TIE fighter.

VANQUISHED BY VADER

The T-16 is no match for a TIE Advanced! When Darth Vader sees it on his tail, he blasts it and sends you crashing to the ground. It's going to be a long, tiring walk back to Uncle Owen's farm!

>> GO BACK AND CHOOSE ANOTHER PATH!

DATA FILE

ETA-2 _ACTIS_-CLASS LIGHT INTERCEPTOR

» Top speed 1,500 kph (900 mph)

» 2 laser cannons

» 2 ion cannons

» Astromech droid socket

You follow Obi-Wan in his superfast red Jedi Interceptor. As soon as you get into space, a message comes through on the comlink—your fully encrypted, long-range communication device. It is from Obi-Wan's fellow Jedi, Anakin Skywalker, who says he can help you. What do you do?

R4-P17 astromech droid

Obi-Wan Kenobi

SAFE SPACE

Although Obi-Wan does not like to fly, his sleek red Interceptor has seen him through many battles and missions. Obi-Wan's astromech droid, R4-P17, provides support.

With Anakin saying he can lead you to the Sith Lord you seek, you set a course to meet up with his ship.

TURN TO
73

OR

Something seems wrong, so you head for Coruscant to see Anakin's mentor, Chancellor Palpatine.

TURN TO
54

Piloting the stolen Imperial shuttle *Tydirium*, you have no trouble getting past the Imperial patrols that encircle the Forest Moon of Endor. You land the shuttle on the remote moon and go in search of the power station you have come to sabotage. Suddenly, you hear a noise in the trees. What is the best thing to do?

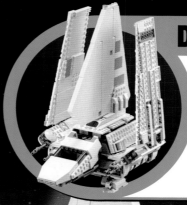

DATA FILE

TYDIRIUM: LAMBDA-CLASS T-4A SHUTTLE

» Top speed 850 kph (528 mph)

» 3 twin laser cannons

» 2 twin blaster cannons

ACCESS ALL AREAS

Sleek Imperial shuttles like the *Tydirium* are used by high-ranking Imperial officers, and even by the Emperor himself. They are equipped with clearance codes that allow them to get past patrols and checkpoints without being searched or questioned.

Quietly investigate the noise —you may have been seen by stormtroopers!

TURN TO **62**

OR

Run away from the noise —you may have been seen by stormtroopers!

TURN TO **58**

JOURNEY TO JEDHA

When the X-wing's coordinates take you to Jedha, you see that it is heavily occupied by Imperial forces, who are mining kyber crystals for weaponry. You go looking for signs of resistance, and soon see two brave warriors—Baze Malbus and Chirrut Îmwe—trying to protect innocent citizens from an Imperial tank. Should you help them or leave them to it?

DATA FILE

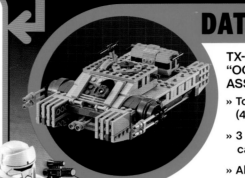

TX-225 GAVW "OCCUPIER" COMBAT ASSAULT TANK

» Top speed 72 kph (45 mph)

» 3 medium laser cannons

» Also transports cargo

Crate of kyber crystals

Chirrut Îmwe

Baze Malbus

Throw yourself into the action. Chirrut and Baze could use your help taking on these troopers!

**TURN TO 90**

OR

Let Chirrut and Baze do their thing. They know what they're up to and you don't want to get in their way!

**TURN TO 81**

STREET FIGHTERS

Before the Empire came to Jedha, Baze Malbus and Chirrut Îmwe were warrior monks who guarded a great temple. Now they do whatever they can to defy the Empire, whose forces patrol the streets in heavy tanks such as this one.

VICIOUS VULTURES

You travel to Coruscant, a huge city planet and the capital of the Galactic Republic. It is the last place you'd expect to be attacked, but as you approach, your ship is ambushed by vulture droids! It takes all your piloting and targeting skill to blast them to bits. Who can help you find out where they came from?

DATA FILE

VULTURE-CLASS STARFIGHTER

» Top speed 1,200 kph (746 mph)

» Twin blaster cannons

» Wings can become legs on the ground

Buzz droid

BUZZ OFF!

Vulture droids are compact spaceships controlled by computer brains instead of pilots. They can launch small sabotage specialists known as buzz droids, which patrol space and attach themselves to nearby vessels, attacking them with cutting tools.

The local police might know who is using buzz droids to patrol the area over Coruscant. Ask them.

TURN TO **95**

OR

The Chancellor is the best-connected person on Coruscant. He is sure to have some ideas. Ask him what he has heard.

TURN TO **54**

After you destroy the droid, you turn to see General Grievous racing past! Grievous is a fearsome cyborg who has replaced bits of his body with machine parts. The bike he is riding looks unstoppable, but a hidden hole in the rocky ground causes it to crash! You, Obi-Wan, and the clone troopers soon have Grievous surrounded. You capture him and question him—but can he be trusted?

DATA FILE

TSMEU-6 WHEEL BIKE

» Top speed 330 kph (205 mph) rolling; 10 kph (6 mph) on legs

» Double laser cannon

» All-terrain vehicle

With his four arms, General Grievous can drive his bike and fight at the same time!

I'M NOT ENJOYING THIS ADVENTURE AT ALL!

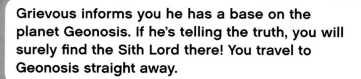

Grievous informs you he has a base on the planet Geonosis. If he's telling the truth, you will surely find the Sith Lord there! You travel to Geonosis straight away.

TURN TO 99

OR

You decide Grievous can't be trusted, and U-3PO finds plans in his bike that suggest he was heading to Kashyyyk! He could be meeting a Sith Lord there. Go to Kashyyyk!

TURN TO 22

ROCK AND ROLL

Grievous's bike can speed along on one giant wheel or gallop on four fold-out legs. Each leg has a clawed foot so it can climb even the steepest slopes of Utapau's rocky surface.

X-WING FIGHTER

The crashed ships are X-wings, a classic rebel craft, but there is no sign of their pilots. They must have ejected to safety! Neither ship is badly damaged, and Luke has a sudden feeling he should fly one to Dagobah. But their computers show they were headed elsewhere. Where will you take your X-wing?

DATA FILE

T-65B X-WING STARFIGHTER

» **Top speed 1,050 kph (652 mph)**

» **4 laser cannons**

» **2 proton torpedo launchers**

WORD ON THE WINGS

The Rebel Alliance uses X-wings in its fight against the Empire. Their name comes from the way they open out to an "X" shape, giving their weapons a wider field of fire.

Follow Luke to the planet Dagobah to find out what is drawing him there.

TURN TO **102**

OR

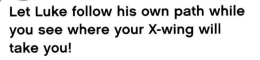

Let Luke follow his own path while you see where your X-wing will take you!

TURN TO **29**

DATA FILE

FIRESPRAY-31-CLASS ATTACK CRAFT

» **Top speed 1,000 kph (620 mph)**

» **Twin rotating blaster cannon**

» **Proton torpedo tubes**

You follow your bounty hunter accomplices to a docking bay, where another bounty hunter, Boba Fett, has snuck aboard in his ship, *Slave I*. Fett usually works on his own but will sometimes work with others, if the pay is high enough! He agrees to give you a lift—but is there a catch?

SIDEWAYS SHIP

Unlike most spacecraft, *Slave I* turns onto its back to land. It flies with its cockpit facing forward, but comes to rest with the pilot facing upward.

You want to find out what Boba Fett is up to, and who he is working for. You go with him to Cloud City.

TURN TO **40**

OR

Some of the bounty hunters are headed to the palace of notorious gangster Jabba the Hutt. Go there instead.

TURN TO **49**

Unkar Plutt gives you directions to the site of the crashed TIE fighter, so you set off. Your choice of transport is a mighty luggabeast. This four-legged, mechanically enhanced creature is slow but steady, and stomps easily across sand dunes. As you travel, a huge sandstorm picks up and you can't see where you're going. What do you do now?

BUILD IT!

No one knows what a luggabeast's head looks like beneath its hood. But they will when you build one! Use tan bricks to match the color of its legs.

Teedo rider

WE'RE DOOMED IF MY SENSORS DON'T WORK!

Luggabeast hood

BEASTS OF BURDEN

The luggabeasts of Jakku are mostly ridden by the Teedo species. These reptilian scavengers build metal hoods and other devices directly onto the creatures' bodies to make the luggabeasts more like machines than animals.

You decide to press on until you reach the TIE fighter crash site. The luggabeast will know the way!

TURN TO **16**

OR

U-3PO thinks it's too dangerous to travel in the sandstorm! You find shelter until it clears.

TURN TO **59**

PRISON BREAK!

When you reach the Death Star prison cells, you hear alarms and blaster fire. You came to find some prisoners, but two daring heroes have beaten you to it! Their names are Luke and Han, and they have just disguised themselves as stormtroopers to rescue rebel Princess Leia. They need your help to get back to Han's ship, but which way is best?

LEIA'S LOCATION

The Death Star's jail has multiple levels for prisoners. Princess Leia is being held on level five of Detention Block AA-23, in cell 2187.

Han Solo

Luke Skywalker

Imperial trooper

Fight your way back to Han's ship, the *Millennium Falcon*, through corridors full of stormtroopers.

TURN TO 83

OR

Sneak back to Han's ship by crawling through the Death Star's garbage chutes. Stinky, but fewer stormtroopers!

TURN TO 55

BUILD IT!

Swap the heads of your minifigures to disguise any character as a stormtrooper—or to give them a new look!

CHASE ON UTAPAU

Quick! You race across Utapau to hunt down General Grievous. You find him, but your two arms are no match for his four—this time! The creepy cyborg can steer his speeder while defending himself with stolen lightsabers in his other hands. Grievous races away to the safety of his ship. Do you dare follow him?

DATA FILE

REPULSORLIFT SPEEDER

» Twin laser cannons

» Rocket launchers

» Thruster exhaust, which is harmless to battle droids

GRIEVOUS'S COMBAT SPEEDER

Utapau is a good place for Grievous to hide from the Jedi hunting him. On this rocky ground he needs a fast, powerful, and agile vehicle capable of attacking oncoming enemies.

You jump into your ship to follow Grievous into space. You are determined to catch this vicious foe!

TURN TO **65**

OR

You will need help if you are going to take on General Grievous's ship. Send a message out to another brave Jedi, Anakin Skywalker.

TURN TO **84**

FORCE FACT!
-- --- --
General Grievous is a fearsome warrior from the planet Kalee. Part man, part machine, he led the Separatist droid army during the Clone Wars.

You sprint toward the distant creature as quickly as you can, hoping its rider can help you. With Tatooine's two suns in your eyes, it is impossible to see clearly until you get up close and realize that the creature is a dewback—and its rider is an Imperial sandtrooper!

FORCE FACT!
-- --- --
The Empire doesn't know it, but Jedi Obi-Wan Kenobi has been living in secret on Tatooine for years. The desert dunes have many caves perfect for hiding in.

SUITED FOR SAND
Dewbacks are huge, green reptiles that live on Tatooine. Sandtroopers use them to get around the desert because they are more reliable than machines, which break when they get sand in their gears and circuits.

C-3PO, I TOLD YOU THAT SPEEDER WAS A BETTER OPTION!

THE DROIDS HE'S LOOKING FOR
Tusken Raiders are bad, but sandtroopers are worse! This one is out searching for your escape pod. He says your droid friends are carrying stolen Imperial data—and now you are all under arrest!

>> GO BACK AND CHOOSE ANOTHER PATH!

Oh no! As you race toward the other speeder, you realize it is surrounded by stormtroopers. It is a First Order patrol piloted by a First Order officer and it is probably looking for the *Falcon*! You start to change direction, but they have already seen you. You could stay and fight, but U-3PO thinks you should step on the gas! What do you do?

DATA FILE

FIRST ORDER SPEEDER

» Repulsorlift engines

» Flametrooper escort

» Rear gunner position

A NEW ORDER

The First Order is a group of fanatics that wants to impose its will on the galaxy. It uses armies of white-armored stormtroopers to crush personal freedom and instill obedience through fear.

First Order officer

Flametroopers, a type of stormtrooper, fire flames from their blasters!

Rear gunner

You hope that your speeder lives up to its name and try to get away as fast as you can.

TURN TO **46**

OR

You feel brave! You stay and fight the First Order using whatever weapons you can find in your speeder.

TURN TO **67**

AWESOME AIRSTRIKE

Just when all seems lost on Geonosis, a huge gunship swoops down with cannons blazing and destroys the enemy droids with just a few blasts! When the ship lands, you discover that two Jedi are aboard: Master Yoda and Anakin Skywalker. Who will you go with to continue your mission?

DATA FILE

LOW ALTITUDE ASSAULT TRANSPORT/INFANTRY
» Top speed 620 kph (385 mph)
» 4 composite-beam ball turrets and 3 laser turrets
» 2 rocket launchers

REPUBLIC GUNSHIP

This large troop transporter and attack craft is designed to travel in a planetary atmosphere, but it can be modified to serve in space as well.

DON'T MIND ME. JUST DESTROY ALL THOSE BATTLE DROIDS!

Padmé Amidala

Anakin Skywalker

Yoda

Yoda is also tracking a Sith Lord on Geonosis. You decide to stick with Jedi Master Yoda.

TURN TO **56**

OR

Anakin Skywalker says he senses the Sith Lord is not on Geonosis. You opt to leave the planet with Anakin.

TURN TO **73**

FORCE FACT!
-- --- --
There are thousands of Jedi in the Galactic Republic. They lead its Grand Army in the battle against the Separatists, commanding vast battalions of clone troopers.

When you get to Cloud City, you can't help but be impressed. A huge sky-station that floats above the planet Bespin, it was built to mine precious gas from the air and freeze it for transport around the galaxy. Boba Fett says you really must see the carbon-freezing chambers while you're here!

FREEZER SECTION

The carbon-freezing chambers of Cloud City are operated by tough, pig-faced Ugnaughts. The chambers are designed to encase Tibanna gas in frozen carbonite, but they can be used to freeze living people, too!

Ugnaught operator

Person in carbonite

CAUGHT IN CARBONITE

It's a trap! Boba Fett has brought you to Cloud City to freeze you in carbonite and sell you back to the Empire. He figures it will pay to get its prisoner back, and will never know that he helped you to escape in the first place!

>> GO BACK AND CHOOSE ANOTHER PATH!

PAGING POE!

U-3PO was right! You find the First Order's communications room and manage to send out a signal. Resistance pilot Poe Dameron picks it up, and leads a strike force of X-wings to attack the Star Destroyer. The attack allows you and your friends to escape in the *Falcon*!

DATA FILE

BLACK ONE T-70 X-WING FIGHTER

» Flown by Captain Poe Dameron

» Copilot is Poe's droid, BB-8

» Coated with sensor-scattering paint

CAPTAIN COURAGEOUS

Poe Dameron is one of General Leia Organa's most trusted Resistance fighters. He is a brave and brilliant pilot, and a good friend to have in a crisis. He claims that he can fly anything, but favors this striking black and orange X-wing.

CALL OFF THE SEARCH

As the *Falcon* joins in the attack, Poe signals from his X-wing to congratulate you. Your distress call has given away the location of the First Order flagship—a vessel the Resistance has been hunting for months!

»» GO BACK AND CHOOSE ANOTHER PATH!

When the landspeeder pilot sees you running toward him, he comes and scares the Tusken Raiders away. He introduces himself as Luke Skywalker. Luke says he can take you to the spaceport in a town named Mos Eisley if you want to leave Tatooine right away, or you could stop off at his place first. Which would you prefer?

DATA FILE

X-34 LANDSPEEDER
» Top speed 250 kph (155 mph)
» 3 air-cooled thrusters
» Repulsorlift engine
» Open cockpit for 2

REPULSORLIFT RUNABOUT

Landspeeders are small vehicles that use repulsorlift engines to hover just above the ground. Most models are cheap and easy to drive, which makes them a popular way to get around in many parts of the galaxy.

NICE TO MEET YOU LUKE! NOW GET ME OUT OF HERE!

Gather your droid friends for a trip to Luke's family farmstead.

TURN TO **12**

OR

Get in the landspeeder and go straight to the spaceport.

TURN TO **88**

A-WING ASSAULT

You take off in a small A-wing fighter and head toward the Forest Moon of Endor. This is where the Imperial power station is based. When you reach orbit, you see just what the station is powering: the shields for an enormous super weapon—the new Death Star!

DATA FILE

RZ-1 A-WING INTERCEPTOR
» Top speed 1,300 kph (808 mph)
» 2 laser cannons
» 12 concussion missiles

BACK TO BASICS

A-wings get their name from their wedge shape, which resembles a capital "A." The ones used by the Rebel Alliance are stripped of their deflector shields, armor plating, and heavy weapons to make them as fast as possible.

END OVER ENDOR

Your tiny starfighter is no match for the might of the Death Star. As the Empire dispatches a squad of TIE fighters to intercept your ship, you wish you'd come here in the stolen Imperial shuttle instead!

>> GO BACK AND CHOOSE ANOTHER PATH!

When you get to Naboo, you are welcomed by two members of the Naboo Royal Security Forces. They say if a Sith Lord is causing trouble there, then Queen Amidala is sure to have heard about it. They offer to take you to her in their flash speeder, but can't agree on the best place to find her! Can you make a decision for them?

DATA FILE

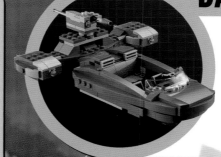

NABOO FLASH SPEEDER

» Floats using repulsorlift engines

» Turret-mounted blaster cannon

» Used for Naboo Security Guard patrols

NEIGHBORS

The planet Naboo is famous for its beauty. Its human population lives on the land and is ruled by Queen Amidala. Another peaceful and intelligent species, the Gungans, lives underwater. It has its own customs and leaders.

> MAYBE WE SHOULD JUST STAY HERE AT THE PALACE?

Go to the Royal Palace. One of the guards thinks the Queen is bound to be there!

TURN TO **61**

OR

Go to the Gungans' underwater city. The other guard is sure she was planning a trip!

TURN TO **75**

FLIGHT OF THE *PHOENIX*

You join some of the brave rebels that make up Phoenix Squadron on their ship, *Phoenix Home*. Their heavily armed ship is huge. With space for a crew of 900, it is often used as the group's headquarters. As you and the rebels set off on a mission to the planet Seelos, a distress call comes in. Should you convince the crew to delay the mission to lend a hand?

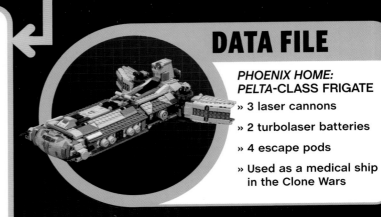

DATA FILE

PHOENIX HOME: PELTA-CLASS FRIGATE

» 3 laser cannons

» 2 turbolaser batteries

» 4 escape pods

» Used as a medical ship in the Clone Wars

EXTRA ENGINES

In normal flight, *Phoenix Home's* two rear wings are folded flat along the hull. But when the ship needs an extra burst of speed, the wings open out to reveal two extra engines on either side of the main thruster.

Carry on to Seelos without stopping. Your help is needed against an Imperial attack.

TURN TO **101**

OR

Someone needs your help! Change course to answer the distress call. You can return to your mission afterward.

TURN TO **66**

TRANSPORTER TROUBLE

You do your best to outrace the stormtroopers, but you have just the one speeder, and unlike them, you can't call on reinforcements! Sweeping around a massive sand dune, you come face to face with a huge First Order transporter. This vehicle is large but also fierce and fast. It quickly lowers its ramp and deploys its troops.

DATA FILE

ATMOSPHERIC ASSAULT LANDER
» **Top speed 900 kph (560 mph)**
» **Blaster cannon**
» **Floodlights to dazzle the enemy**

30 SECONDS TO SURFACE

Also known as AALs, First Order transporters can carry troops from an orbiting spacecraft to a planet's surface in less than 30 seconds. Each transporter has room for 20 troopers, a gunner, and a pilot.

NO ESCAPE!

With the transporter in front of you and the speeder patrol not far behind, there is nothing you can do to escape from the First Order. As you are taken prisoner, you wish you had put up a fight when you had the chance!

» GO BACK AND CHOOSE ANOTHER PATH!

BATTLE DROID ARMY

You help the Wookiees hold back the battle droids, but they just keep on coming! It looks like the droid army is winning—until Commander Gree stomps into battle on his powerful All Terrain Attack Pod (AT-AP). This fast, three-legged walker can destroy many battle droids with just one shot. The droid army is soon on the retreat! What's your next move?

DATA FILE

ALL TERRAIN ATTACK POD

» Top speed 60 kph (37 mph)

» Long-range blaster

» Laser cannon

Commander Gree

Super battle droid

Battle droid commander

CLONE COMMANDER

The clone trooper in charge of this AT-AP is Commander Gree. Like all members of the clone army, he is a duplicate of the bounty hunter Jango Fett.

Wookiee leader Chief Tarfful

There are reports of more attacks. You head back to base with Gree to help plan for the next battle.

TURN TO **89**

OR

You are confident that Gree and the clone troopers can hold off the battle droid attacks. You continue your search for the Sith Lord in space.

TURN TO **27**

JUST IN TIME, COMMANDER GREE!

The scout troopers weren't expecting you to run at them! Their bikes cannot change direction so quickly, so the troopers are forced to swerve to avoid crashing into you. Two of their speeder bikes go veering off into the trees, but that still leaves three troopers in control of their bikes. They turn and draw their blasters…

DATA FILE

74-Z SPEEDER BIKE

» Top speed 500 kph (311 mph)

» Rotating blaster cannon

» Used by Imperials but sometimes stolen by rebels

SKILLS OF A SCOUT

Imperial scout troopers wear lighter armor than stormtroopers, and are trained to carry out more complex missions. They have the fast reflexes needed to pilot speeder bikes, and can survive using their wits in remote, hostile environments.

SO NEAR AND YET SO FAR!

The scout troopers take you straight to the bunker you have come to destroy, but there is nothing you can do under their watchful gaze! You were so close to ending the Empire forever… but what could you have done differently?

» GO BACK AND CHOOSE ANOTHER PATH!

Jabba the Hutt's palace is well protected, but you have no trouble getting in, thanks to your bounty hunter allies. They often work for the gruesome gangster, so are welcomed as old friends. However, when Jabba sees you, he demands to know who you are and what you want in his palace. What will you tell him?

BUILD IT!

Jabba's palace has many different rooms including dungeons and guards' quarters. How many can you build?

Frozen Han Solo

Jabba

VISITING SOMEONE'S HOUSE WITHOUT BRINGING A PRESENT? BAD IDEA!

Jabba's servants

There's no turning back now! Step forward and say you have come to honor the galaxy's greatest gangster!

TURN TO
53

OR

Hang back and say you have come here by mistake, and ask if someone can kindly show you the exit... please?

TURN TO
17

HORRIBLE HUTT

Jabba the Hutt is a huge, slug-like crime lord. He lives in luxury on the planet Tatooine, surrounded by servants and advisors who live in fear of upsetting him.

The X-wing leads you here, a First Order base built into an icy planet. This is Starkiller Base—the First Order's latest superweapon—and the Resistance wants to blow it up! You fly the ship close to the base and start to attack, but the base is heavily guarded. Laser fire brings you crashing down, and you are soon surrounded by snowtroopers!

DATA FILE

LIGHT INFANTRY UTILITY VEHICLE

» Also known as First Order snowspeeder

» Top speed 250 kph (150 mph)

» Repeating blaster weapon

TROOPING ON ICE

First Order snowtroopers wear special armor to keep them warm in freezing conditions, and drive snowspeeders to navigate icy lands. Their capes keep ice out of their armor joints, and the narrow eye slits in their helmets protect them from the snow's reflective glare.

I DON'T KNOW WHAT'S WORSE— SANDY CIRCUITS OR FROZEN CIRCUITS!

CAPTURED IN THE SNOW

The laser blast came from a First Order snowspeeder —one of several now training their weapons on you! There's no way out for you and U-3PO, and you wish you hadn't raced here alone!

>> GO BACK AND CHOOSE ANOTHER PATH!

POWER TO THE PALACE

The palace power generator provides energy for Naboo's capital city, Theed. One of its most important functions is to supply plasma to power the city's starfighters. That's why the generator is right beside the palace hangar.

Your chase leads you into Theed Palace and through a door into the palace power generator. This huge power plant is a dangerous place, but with Obi-Wan at your side you are able to avoid the many plasma pits and force fields. Eventually you come face to face with the mysterious Sith Lord Darth Maul on the edge of a plasma pit. Here you prepare for battle!

Plasma pit

DOWN AND OUT

Darth Maul is a fierce fighter, but with Obi-Wan's help you plunge him into the oblivion of a plasma pit! Naboo—and the whole galaxy—is saved from whatever scheme Maul was plotting, and you are suddenly a hero of the Republic!

>> GO BACK AND CHOOSE ANOTHER PATH!

Luke is a skilled pilot! As you watch him perform amazing tricks in his T-16 skyhopper, you spot three other ships fighting in the distance. One lets loose a volley of lasers, then flies off as the other two crash-land in a sand dune. What should you do?

BUILD IT!

Tatooine is home to strange desert creatures such as dewbacks, womp rats, and krayt dragons. What other alien animals could you build?

DATA FILE

T-16 SKYHOPPER

» **Top speed 1,200 kph (746 mph)**

» **Pneumatic cannon**

» **Repulsorlift engine**

FREQUENT FLYER

The T-16 skyhopper is a popular form of short-distance transport on many different worlds. Luke likes to fly his T-16 through Tatooine's desert canyons, using its cannon to practice his shooting skills as he goes.

Convince Luke to chase after the escaping ship in the T-16, hoping to bring its pilot to justice.

TURN TO **26**

OR

Get Luke to land the skyhopper by the crashed ships so that you can try to help the pilots.

TURN TO **32**

INTO THE PIT!

You boldly step forward to address Jabba, but he just grins and pulls a lever. This opens a trapdoor that is hidden in Jabba's palace floor. He never was going to let you speak—he just wanted the amusement of seeing you fall into his rancor pit!

Rancor

Malakili is the rancor's keeper

One of Jabba's Gamorrean guards

ER... DID I MENTION? DROIDS AREN'T VERY TASTY...

INTO THE PET!

Far below Jabba's throne room, you find yourself at the feet of his enormous pet rancor. It's a long time since the beast had breakfast, and you realize you are about to become pet food!

>> GO BACK AND CHOOSE ANOTHER PATH!

A HUTT'S BEST FRIEND

Rancors are huge reptiles with long, clawed fingers and fang-filled mouths. Jabba the Hutt keeps one as a pet and lets it eat his enemies—and anyone else that annoys him!

Chancellor Palpatine welcomes you as you enter his grand office at the heart of Coruscant. He wields great power as the head of the Galactic Republic, and is popular across the galaxy. But Obi-Wan is still at your side, and his sense of an evil presence is now stronger than ever. Could Palpatine be the Sith Lord you are looking for?

ANSWER THE QUESTION: ARE YOU A SITH LORD, YES OR NO?

Chancellor Palpatine

Yes—you're certain. The Sith Lord must be Palpatine! Convince Obi-Wan that you must challenge him together.

TURN TO **57**

OR

No, it couldn't be the Chancellor—could it? Tell Obi-Wan that you need to find proof.

TURN TO **80**

SUPREME POWER

The Chancellor of the Republic is the galaxy's chief decision maker and sets laws that everyone has to obey. In his time as Chancellor, Palpatine has gained more power than any one person should have.

55

STRAIGHT IN THE GARBAGE!

With stormtroopers firing at you from every direction, you dive headfirst into a garbage chute. Luke, Han, and Leia follow you, as does their Wookiee pal, Chewbacca. These trash tunnels link up all over the Death Star. It should be possible to get anywhere from here. However, there are garbage mashers inside and monsters known as dianogas lurking underneath…

THE TROUBLE WITH TRASH

With more than a million people aboard, the Death Star has a serious waste problem! This is solved by sending all the trash to huge chambers with moving walls, where everything is squashed into compact blocks.

Dianoga eyestalk

A COMPRESSED CONCLUSION

Uh-oh! The sorting sensors think you are organic waste and tip you into a garbage masher! As the walls close in around you and your friends and the dianoga's tentacles rise up from below the trash, you wish you had taken your chances with the stormtroopers!

>> GO BACK AND CHOOSE ANOTHER PATH!

You follow Yoda across Geonosis. Yoda is the wise Grand Master of the Jedi Order and has trained many Jedi over hundreds of years. He is far more powerful than his size would suggest. Suddenly, you hear a "beep-beep." What's that coming in over the comlink? Yoda tells you he has tracked down the Sith Lord Count Dooku. You have finally found the Sith, but what is your next move?

DATA FILE

ETA-2 *ACTIS*-CLASS LIGHT INTERCEPTOR
» Top speed 1,250 kph (775 mph)
» 2 laser cannons
» Astromech droid socket

YODA'S CREST

Yoda's modified Jedi interceptor is decorated with his unique crest on each wing. This helps other Jedi to identify his ship.

R2-D2 is helping Yoda on his mission

Yoda

You will find Count Dooku's ship as it prepares to land on Geonosis, and launch an air attack.

TURN TO **105**

OR

You plan to wait for Dooku's ship to land so that you can battle him on the ground.

TURN TO **118**

BUILD IT!

Build a starship with a socket for a handy astromech droid. Make sure the droid can peek out to keep an eye on flight performance.

A SWIFT EXIT

Just as you and Obi-Wan draw your weapons to challenge Palpatine, the Chancellor unleashes a bolt of Force lightning that hurls you both to the ground! Palpatine flees for the door at one side of his office, through which he keeps a private shuttle, ready to take off at a moment's notice.

CLONE CREW

Chancellor Palpatine is far too important to fly his own shuttle! He has a small crew of clone troopers standing by, ready to launch the fast and powerful ship whenever he demands it.

DATA FILE

THETA-CLASS T-2C PERSONNEL TRANSPORT

» Top speed 2,000 kph (1,243 mph)

» 2 quad laser cannons

» Wings fold for landing

THE SITH REVEALED!

You were right: Palpatine is the Sith Lord you were looking for! But as you watch him fly away, you realize that you have no way to prove it. Your eagerness to fight has given him a chance to escape and to cover his evil tracks.

>> GO BACK AND CHOOSE ANOTHER PATH!

DEATH STAR DEFENSE

The Imperial power station is housed in a heavily armored bunker. It generates the shields that surround and protect the Empire's greatest weapon—the Death Star— while it is being built in orbit of Endor.

As you run deeper into the forest, you blunder into the clearing where the power station is located! This is your chance to disable the Death Star. However, the entrance is being guarded by stormtroopers, who call for reinforcements when they see you. Closing in on either side are an AT-ST walker and a squad of scout troopers on speeder bikes. What can you do?

BUILD IT!

The Forest Moon of Endor is covered in forests full of huge, ancient trees. What is the biggest LEGO tree you can build?

HOW ABOUT OPTION 3: HIDE IN THE SHIELD BUNKER?

 Run toward the AT-ST—it is a slower opponent than the speeder bikes. TURN TO **21**

OR

 Head for the scout troopers— they are less powerful than the AT-ST. TURN TO **48**

ABANDONED X-WING

As you shelter from the sandstorm, you realize that you have parked yourself next to an empty X-wing! These reliable ships are commonly used by the Resistance and flown by pilots wearing orange flight suits. There is no sign of this X-wing's pilot, but inside you see the ship is still working and you jump in. Where do you fly to?

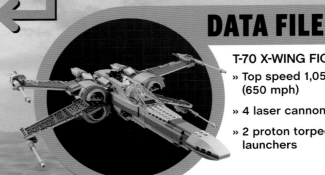

DATA FILE

T-70 X-WING FIGHTER

» Top speed 1,050 kph (650 mph)

» 4 laser cannons

» 2 proton torpedo launchers

NOW WE CAN FINALLY GET OFF THIS DUSTY PLANET!

NEXT-GENERATION X

T-70 X-wings like this one are at the forefront of the Resistance's fight against the First Order. This version is faster and more powerful than the X-wings once flown by the Rebel Alliance— and is available in more colors!

Some coordinates are still programmed into the X-wing's computer. They must be important! You decide to follow them.

TURN TO **50**

OR

You feel certain the sandstorm will have distracted the First Order. You fly the X-wing back to your friends on board the *Falcon*.

TURN TO **78**

BUILD IT!

Use sloped and angled pieces to build an aerodynamic X-wing and choose your own color theme to personalize it!

Never ignore an Imperial ship! When you try to run instead of replying, it comes racing after you with its laser cannon blazing. To your dismay, you see it is a heavily armored Imperial assault carrier—delivering a cargo of TIE fighters to the Star Destroyer you just escaped from!

DATA FILE

GOZANTI-CLASS CRUISER

» Top speed 1,025 kph (635 mph)

» Twin laser turret

» Heavy laser cannon

HEAVY CARGO

The Empire uses assault carriers to deliver other ships and vehicles into battle. They mostly carry TIE fighters on docking clamps beneath their wings, but can also transport enormous AT-ATs.

BACK THE WAY YOU CAME

The assault carrier scores a direct hit on your ion engines and ensnares you in its tractor beam. As it resumes course for the Star Destroyer, you are towed behind as just another piece of cargo! The Imperial forces will be pleased to see you again…

» GO BACK AND CHOOSE ANOTHER PATH!

PERIL IN THE PALACE

The Naboo Security Guards' flash speeder enters the Royal Palace through the grand hangar—home of the sleekest starfighters on Naboo. You see no sign of Queen Amidala here, but you do see... the Sith Lord Darth Maul! When he sees you, he runs for his ship. Can you catch him here, or should you take him on in the air?

DATA FILE

NABOO ROYAL N-1 STARFIGHTER
» Top speed 1,100 kph (684 mph)
» 2 blaster cannons
» Proton torpedoes

FORCE FACT!
-- --- --
Darth Maul is a mighty dark side warrior who hates the Jedi! He fights with a double-bladed lightsaber known as a saberstaff.

The starfighters are famed for their speed! Jump into one to battle Darth Maul in the air.

TURN TO **87**

OR

You'd rather cut Darth Maul off before he can reach his ship. Chase after him to catch him on the ground.

TURN TO **51**

FLYING COLORS

With their elegant curves and bright yellow finish, Naboo starfighters are designed for display as much as defense. Because Naboo is such a peaceful world, they are used more for parades than anything else!

When you check out the strange noise from among the trees, you come face to face with a small, furry creature holding a spear! As it runs away, U-3PO tells you it is an Ewok —a member of a primitive tribe that lives on the Forest Moon of Endor. Intrigued, you follow it to a wooden village in the treetops. Suddenly there are Ewoks with spears all around you! How will you react?

BUILD IT!

Use brown bricks and other earth-colored elements to build Ewok treehouse forts and tools, such as catapults, gliders, and battering rams.

> I THINK THESE EWOKS REALLY DO LIKE ME!

y to fight the Ewoks so that you can get with your mission. How fierce can the ddly critters really be?

R

TURN TO **70**

y to befriend the Ewoks and explore e Ewok village. Maybe they can help u with your mission to find the Imperial wer station!

TURN TO **113**

TRIBE IN THE TREES

Ewoks are skilled in hunting and building complex tools out of wood, but have no advanced technology. Instead, they use basic, but effective, tools—such as sticks, stones, spears, and catapults. Their treetop villages can be found across Endor's moon.

RELEASE THE RATHTARS!

You travel endless corridors to reach the Star Destroyer's cargo hold. You had hoped the ship might be carrying explosives, but what you find is better: a horde of ravenous rathtars. These vicious carnivores will eat anything—including members of the First Order and the Resistance! You release them, sending stormtroopers flying.

MONSTER MOUTHS

A rathtar is a scary mass of teeth and tentacles! Rathtars hunt in fast-moving packs and are very hard to catch—making them highly prized by scientists and rich collectors.

A GREAT ESCAPE

As you and your friends run back to the *Falcon* and escape, everyone on the Star Destroyer is too distracted to notice! U-3PO says if one of the rathtars eats Kylo Ren, you'll be the galaxy's greatest hero!

>> GO BACK AND CHOOSE ANOTHER PATH!

You follow the Jawas to their huge, rolling home, which U-3PO says is called a sandcrawler. Inside, you see a hive of industry, with magnetic cranes and conveyor belts sorting old and broken machinery into different piles. You look around at your droid companions and wonder why the Jawas offered you a ride...

DATA FILE

GIANT SCAVENGER TANK
» Salvage suction tubes
» Mineral smashers
» Awesome ore crushers
» Can carry 1,500 droids

DESERTED IN THE DESERT

Tatooine's Jawas are small, hooded, and mysterious. They comb the deserts in enormous sandcrawlers looking for old droids and other machinery that they can repair, reprogram, and sell.

BLAST MY MAGNETIC PERSONALITY!

THE JAWAS OF DEFEAT

As the huge door of the sandcrawler clangs shut, you realize that the Jawas have brought you aboard solely to steal your droid friends! You will remain their prisoner until they have sold them for profit!

>> GO BACK AND CHOOSE ANOTHER PATH!

Your pursuit of General Grievous doesn't last long. All of a sudden you come up against the *Malevolence*—Grievous's huge battleship. It is several kilometers long, has 500 turbolasers, and carries a crew of 900 battle droids! With Grievous aboard, it is the flagship of the vast Separatist Navy, ready to take on any ship in the Galactic Republic—including yours.

DATA FILE

SUBJUGATOR-CLASS HEAVY CRUISER

» 2 ion cannons

» 500 turbolasers

» Secondary laser cannons

Ion cannon

ION GIANT

The *Malevolence*'s two enormous ion cannons fire ionized particles. The particles disrupt the electrical systems of nearby ships, leaving them defenseless against laser fire.

MALEVOLENT *MALEVOLENCE*

Your small starfighter is no match for the *Malevolence*! One blast from its huge ion cannons would be enough to shut down your ship's computer systems, leaving you floating helplessly in space just waiting to be captured! Retreat is the only option.

>> GO BACK AND CHOOSE ANOTHER PATH!

You track the distress call to its source and find a Wookiee ship broken down on a barren moon. As you work with the Wookiees to repair their ship, you learn that they have just escaped from an Imperial-occupied planet, Kessel. The Wookiees could be useful to the rebel cause. What should you do?

DATA FILE

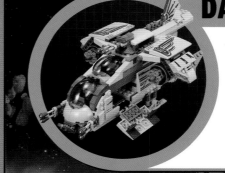

AUZITUCK ANTI-SLAVER GUNSHIP

» Top speed 950 kph (590 mph)

» 3 twin laser cannons

» Interior made from wroshyr trees

WHICH WAY WILL THE WOOKIEES WANDER?

BRAVERY AND SLAVERY

Wookiees are brave and loyal warriors from the planet Kashyyyk. The Empire hunts them down to use as slave labor, so they build unique gunships to protect themselves against being captured, imprisoned, and sold.

Persuade the Wookiees to join you at a rebel hideout on the planet Hoth. You should be safe there!

TURN TO 14

OR

Keep traveling with *Phoenix Home* as it heads off to report back to the rebel fleet at its base.

TURN TO 5

RESISTANCE RESCUE

Rey's speeder is no match for a squad of stormtroopers, but you're not going down without a fight! The sound of battle attracts the attention of a nearby Resistance ship that soon comes to your aid. This transporter is armed with more than enough weapons to send the stormtroopers running! It can hold twenty Resistance fighters—with room for you too. Where should you go?

DATA FILE

RESISTANCE TRANSPORT

» Heavy laser cannon

» Proton torpedo launcher

» Optional ion cannon

BUILT FROM BITS

The Resistance cobbles together its transport ships from bits of other craft. This one has the cockpit of an old B-wing fighter, the body of a freighter, and engines from fifty-year-old Republic-era shuttles!

Detachable pod

You thank the Resistance fighters for their help and ask them to chase after the troopers. You think you can beat them!

TURN TO **108**

OR

You would rather get far away from Jakku! Join the Resistance fighters on their planned trip to the planet Takodana.

TURN TO **98**

BUILD IT!

Be like the Resistance and make something totally new out of three of your LEGO® Star Wars™ vehicle sets!

TAUNTAUN TREK

As the Imperial invasion heats up, you dodge falling rocks and melting ice to get Luke to the tauntaun pens. Here, you saddle up and ride your tauntaun out into the snow. The creature is fast and, unlike a snowspeeder, won't show up on Imperial sensors. However, it only has two legs and no engine—so only gets a short distance before it needs to stop and rest.

Rebel troopers wrap up warmly when riding tauntauns on Hoth.

REBEL RIDES

Tauntauns are large, furry lizards that live in packs on the planet Hoth. The rebels have trained some tauntauns to serve as transport on the planet's slippery surface. They are sure-footed creatures, but also very smelly!

ACTUALLY, I THINK I'D RATHER WALK!

STUCK IN THE SNOW

As the tired tauntaun takes a break, you turn back and see Imperial snowtroopers heading your way on speeder bikes. You can't escape them, and wish you'd taken a speedy snowspeeder from the base instead!

>> GO BACK AND CHOOSE ANOTHER PATH!

MEET THE SPECTRES

You hold on tight as Kanan races out of Lothal City to rejoin his rebel friends. When you tell them how you escaped from the Empire, they invite you to join their crew, the Spectres. There is much work to be done! Kanan thinks you would be perfect for a mission with Phoenix Squadron. They are one of the largest groupings of rebels in the galaxy. Which group will you join?

TALENTED TEAM

Each of the Spectres has a special skill. Kanan and Ezra are Force sensitive, Hera is an ace pilot, Sabine is a weapons expert, and Zeb is a skilled fighter. Chopper, their droid, is just... Chopper!

WHAT A FRIENDLY BUNCH OF FACES! WELL, APART FROM THAT DROID...

Sabine Wren

Chopper (C1-10P)

Kanan Jarrus

Ezra Bridger

Zeb Orrelios

Hera Syndulla

U-3PO likes the Spectres. Accept their offer and leave Lothal with them on their ship, the *Ghost*.

TURN TO **97**

OR

Report for a mission with the Spectres' rebel friends in Phoenix Squadron. You've heard their ship is awesome!

TURN TO **45**

DATA FILE

614-AVA SPEEDER BIKE

» 2 blaster cannons

» Former Imperial speeder

» Custom paintwork by Ezra Bridger

You let out a roar and shake a stick at the Ewoks, but they are not so easily spooked! Ewoks will defend their home against forces that seem both bigger and stronger than them—including you! They march you to a campfire. You hope they are going to feed you, but U-3PO understands their language, and he explains that they want to cook you!

BUILD IT!

Make an oversized U-3PO model for the Ewoks to use as an idol. Decorate it with flowers and other tributes from the forest.

ESSENTIAL EWOKESE

While most intelligent species in the galaxy speak a language called Basic, the isolated Ewoks speak only Ewokese. Handy Ewokese phrases include "Yaa-yaah" (Hello), "Ee chee wa maa!" (That's cool!), and "Yub nub!" (Hooray!).

CHATTING AROUND THE CAMPFIRE

You never thought your mission would end like this! Surrounded by hungry Ewoks, your only hope is U-3PO. The Ewoks think he is one of their sacred idols, so they will surely listen to him… won't they? But for now, there's no escape.

>> GO BACK AND CHOOSE ANOTHER PATH!

FOREST ATTACK

You head into the forests of Kashyyyk with Obi-Wan. But without a Wookiee guide, you quickly take a wrong turn and walk straight into the path of a huge droid gunship! Heavily armed with missiles and laser cannons, it also drops squadrons of battle droids onto its enemies. It's a dangerous craft to encounter!

DATA FILE

HEAVY MISSILE PLATFORM DROID GUNSHIP

» Also know as the Predator

» 7 laser cannons

» Advanced droid brain

» Drops squadrons of battle droids

B2 super battle droid

B1 battle droid

CAUGHT ON KASHYYYK

With no Wookiees in sight, you realize you have crossed enemy lines and are now in Separatist territory. All you can do is allow yourself to be taken prisoner and hope Obi-Wan has a plan up his sleeve. If only you'd agreed to help those Wookiees!

>> GO BACK AND CHOOSE A NEW PATH!

B FOR BATTLE DROID

The gunship deploys a range of droids in battle, such as the B1 battle droid, the B2 super battle droid, and BX-series droid commandos.

Kanan's speeder bike swerves into the alleyway and away from the stormtroopers. But instead of flying to safety, you fly straight into the path of an AT-DP! These two-legged walkers are a common sight on the streets of Lothal, but that doesn't make them any less scary! Their Imperial crews are always looking for chances to spread fear with the AT-DP's huge, stomping feet.

DATA FILE

ALL TERRAIN DEFENSE POD

» Top speed 90 kph (55 mph)

» Heavy laser cannon

» Room for one pilot and one gunner

LOOKS LIKE THAT SHORTCUT WAS A BAD IDEA...

OUTNUMBERED!

You and Kanan begin a brave attack on the AT-DP, but as more Imperial troops arrive your only choice is to surrender. Kanan promises the other Spectres will rescue you eventually, but for now your adventures are over!

>> GO BACK AND CHOOSE ANOTHER PATH!

STANDING STRONG

The legs of an AT-DP may be thin, but they are very strong and stable. It takes a well-placed thermal detonator or a powerful disruptor rifle to bring an AT-DP tumbling to the ground.

ANAKIN IN SPACE

Anakin informs you he can lead you to a Sith Lord! You follow Anakin in his Jedi Interceptor, which displays the red and yellow symbols of his fleet. Obi-Wan tells you he fears Anakin is turning to the dark side of the Force. The dark side values destructive power over patience and wisdom. Who do you trust?

R2-D2 in droid socket

DATA FILE

ETA-2 *ACTIS*-CLASS LIGHT INTERCEPTOR

» Top speed 1,500 kph (900 mph)

» Two laser cannons

» Socket for astromech droid copilot

RISK-TAKER AT LARGE

Anakin is a skilled pilot. This Interceptor is extremely agile, allowing Anakin to fly at speed—often in a reckless way that worries his Jedi Master, Obi-Wan Kenobi!

You trust Obi-Wan's instincts. You agree to challenge Anakin as soon as you reach your destination.

TURN TO 115

OR

You're not sure if you can trust Anakin, but if he says he can lead you to a Sith Lord, it's worth taking the risk!

TURN TO 92

Your Imperial impersonation attempt works—the other ship accepts your reply and continues on its way. You land the TIE fighter on the Imperial-occupied planet Lothal, but it soon attracts attention again. When a couple of stormtroopers get too close, a rebel called Kanan whisks you away on his speeder bike. How can you repay him?

DATA FILE

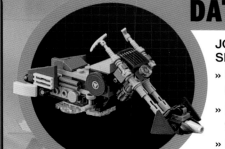

JOBEN T-85 SPEEDER BIKE

» Named after famous racer Thall Joben

» Moll K-19 power generator engine

» Dusat EMP emitter

Cargo cube

KANAN AND COMPANY

Jedi Kanan Jarrus is part of the rebel group called the Spectres. At first, they opposed the Empire solely on Lothal, where the Empire started building weapons factories, but in time they joined up with the wider Rebellion.

JUST GET US OUT OF HERE AS FAST AS POSSIBLE!

Help Kanan by keeping quiet and not distracting him from his route!

TURN TO **69**

OR

Help Kanan by pointing out a shortcut down an alleyway that he can speed along.

TURN TO **72**

The flash speeder gets you to the water's edge, and a submarine takes you the rest of the way to the Gungans' underwater city, Otoh Gunga. There, you meet Queen Amidala. She says she knows nothing about a Sith Lord, but there is another crisis on Naboo. A droid army is attacking the Gungans. Can you help them fight back?

DATA FILE

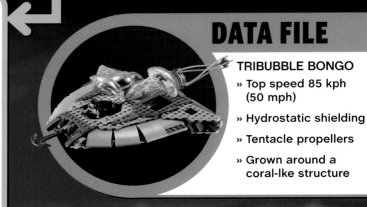

TRIBUBBLE BONGO
» Top speed 85 kph (50 mph)
» Hydrostatic shielding
» Tentacle propellers
» Grown around a coral-lke structure

Queen Amidala

Gungan soldier

Of course you can help the Gungans—Sith hunting can wait until later!

TURN TO
103

OR

There is no time to get involved here—there is still a Sith Lord on the loose!

TURN TO
79

NATIVES OF NABOO

The amphibious Gungans are strong swimmers, but also use submarines to get around. The unusual hulls of these vessels are grown rather than built, and provide a defense against massive sea monsters!

INSIDE THE SUPERLASER!

The Death Star has many corridors, but you eventually find a room full of complex controls and computers. You see technicians wearing special helmets to protect them from laser beams and realize this must be superlaser control! You sit down at a data terminal and think about what to do next.

Imperial gunner

WHO ARE YOU CALLING SUPER LAZY?

MAJOR LASER

The Death Star's superlaser can blow up an entire planet. It is powered by a massive hypermatter reactor and a vast number of powerful kyber crystals—the same rare minerals that are used to make lightsabers.

MSE (mouse) droid

Imperial weapons technician

BY THE SEAT OF YOUR PANTS!

As you sit down, the superlaser jumps into life. You must have perched on a vital button! The superlaser blasts out into the emptiness of space until the Death Star is completely drained of power. Suddenly, the galaxy's greatest weapon is no threat to anyone and it's all thanks to you (and your butt)!

>> GO BACK AND CHOOSE ANOTHER PATH!

As you venture out from the base, you can tell you are catching up with whoever is making the footprints, as they are becoming fresher. In fact, they are fresh enough for you to be sure—these tracks were made by a wampa! These huge, hairy beasts roam the snowy wastes of Hoth, and are often very hungry!

GOOD BOY! NICE WAMPA!

HUNTERS OF HOTH

Wampas are camouflaged with white fur. This makes them hard to see in the snow, where they hunt for food to take back to their frozen cave larders.

AN ABOMINABLE END

You look up from the footprints and see the creature that made them looming over you! With a swipe of its huge paw, the wampa grabs you and drags you off to its cave. You are now even more lost than Luke!

>> GO BACK AND CHOOSE ANOTHER PATH!

Your plan has worked! By the time you get back to the *Falcon*, the First Order has given up looking for you. Reunited with Rey and Chewbacca, you discuss what to do with the X-wing. You all agree to complete its mission for the Resistance. The Resistance has learned of a new First Order base named Starkiller Base, so you fly there with the X-wing and the *Falcon*.

STAR POWER

Starkiller Base is a planet turned into a giant weapon, heavily guarded by First Order forces. Beneath its icy surface, the energy from stars is being collected and stored. Eventually, it will have the power to blast across the galaxy as a planet-destroying beam!

X HITS THE SPOT

At Starkiller Base, the *Falcon* keeps the guards busy with a fake attack while you fly straight to its weak spot and fire. The base is destroyed and you speed away to celebrate with your friends! Excellent teamwork has led to your victory.

>> GO BACK AND CHOOSE ANOTHER PATH!

BATTLE DROID BONANZA!

You wish the Gungans luck in their battle and say goodbye to the underwater city. But as soon as you come ashore, you see the landscape is crawling with battle droids and their Multi-Troop Transports! These floating tanks carry more than 100 battle droids each, and it isn't long before you are surrounded!

BUILT FOR BATTLE

Battle droids are not the smartest soldiers, but they obey orders without question and can be deployed quickly in overwhelming numbers. They also fold away for easy storage in the MTTs that deliver them into battle!

DATA FILE

MULTI-TROOP TRANSPORT (MTT)

» 112-droid complement

» Can also carry super battle droids

» Twin blaster cannons

DEFEATED BY DROIDS

In your quest for the Sith, you have failed to spot the evil right in front of your eyes! MTTs are encircling the Gungan city, and now you are too far away to help them—or for them to help you. You have no choice but to surrender!

>> GO BACK AND CHOOSE ANOTHER PATH!

YOU LOT GIVE DROIDS A BAD NAME!

As soon as you leave Palpatine's office to find proof, you hear a commotion coming from inside. Rushing back in, you see that Separatist droids and tri-fighters have smashed their way in and are taking him prisoner! Palpatine asks for your help, but you let the droids cuff him before you attack and destroy them.

DATA FILE

DROID TRI-FIGHTER
» Built-in droid brain
» No need for a pilot
» 4 laser cannons
» Fires proton torpedoes

THREE-PRONGED ATTACK

Though they look like spaceships, tri-fighters are actually flying droids with built-in weapons. They are used by the Separatists in their battle against the Galactic Empire and named for their three-winged structure.

THE SITH SLIP-UP!

You wanted proof that Palpatine was a Sith Lord, and now he has provided it! The attack was a fake, set up by Palpatine himself to prove he was a good guy and not involved with the Separatists. But you sensed evil and you were not fooled. Now Palpatine is your prisoner. Good job!

» GO BACK AND CHOOSE ANOTHER PATH!

FORCE FACT!
The Separatists broke away from the Republic to form a new alliance. Palpatine secretly controls both sides and has made them go to battle!

SHUTTLE SHUTDOWN

Without you or anyone else helping Chirrut and Baze, their battle against the Imperial tank goes on long enough for reinforcements to arrive. As you hang back, you see a scary-looking shuttle approaching Jedha. Imperial rule is heavy in this corner of the galaxy and you have now become separated and are without backup!

DATA FILE

DELTA-CLASS T-3C SHUTTLE

» Top speed 970 kph (603 mph)

» 2 sets of laser cannons

» 2 wingtip cannons

» Huge folding wings

MEET THE ELITE

This shuttle belongs to Director Orson Krennic, a high-ranking Imperial officer in charge of building the Empire's Death Star weapon. Aboard, he is accompanied by his personal squad of elite stormtroopers, known as death troopers, who are feared galaxy-wide for their expert combat skills.

CAUGHT BY KRENNIC

Orson Krennic is under pressure from the Empire to crush rebel uprisings. He is not happy to see resistance to Imperial rule on Jedha. He is quick to catch you and says you will be imprisoned for a very long time!

>> GO BACK AND CHOOSE ANOTHER PATH!

Aboard the Resistance Bomber you meet Rey's friend Finn and his new pal, Rose. Finn was raised to be a stormtrooper, but ran away from the First Order and teamed up with the Resistance. Now he and Rose are going off on a very important secret mission. They offer to drop you off somewhere first, though. Where will you choose to go?

DATA FILE

RESISTANCE TRANSPORT POD

» Two-seater cockpit, plus space for droid

» Side-mounted blasters

» Tail fin for stability at high speed

TROOPER NO MORE

Ex-stormtrooper Finn flies a small gray and orange Resistance ship with Rose. The craft receives navigation advice from the droid BB-8.

You have heard that rebels are welcome on the peaceful planet Takodana, so you travel there.

TURN TO **98**

OR

You would like to continue the fight with the Resistance forces so you try to catch up with their bomber, which was headed to the planet Crait.

TURN TO **20**

BUILD IT!

Make your own escape pod or transporter from as few parts as possible. Don't forget a cockpit shield. A fin will make your ship aerodynamic.

"This is the *Millennium Falcon*!" says smuggler Han Solo as you see his ship for the first time. After your adventures, it's a sight for sore eyes—even though Han's huge Wookiee copilot, Chewbacca, seems scary! Han boasts that this is the fastest ship in the galaxy and he could take you anywhere. Where do you want to go?

DATA FILE

MILLENNIUM FALCON: YT-1300F LIGHT FREIGHTER

» Top speed 1,050 kph (652 mph)

» 2 quad laser cannons

» Tractor beam projectors

Persuade Han to join up with the rebel fleet—you're ready to take the fight to the Empire!

TURN TO 5

Ask to go to a rebel base— somewhere the Empire is very unlikely to find you.

TURN TO 14

ROGUE TWO

Han Solo and Chewbacca are smugglers who just want to make a living while steering clear of stormtroopers. Han has upgraded the *Millennium Falcon* many times over the years, so the two rogues can evade most Imperial ships.

Anakin Skywalker joins your hunt for Grievous in his sleek Delta-7 starfighter. The ace Jedi pilot has customized his ship to be faster than other Jedi craft. Before you can all catch up with Grievous, you come under attack from Sith apprentice Asajj Ventress! With Anakin's help, you manage to escape, but you realize that a powerful Sith must have sent Ventress. Who do you talk to first?

DATA FILE

DELTA-7 JEDI INTERCEPTOR

» Dual laser cannons and proton torpedoes

» Detachable escape pod

» Astromech navigation

Asajj Ventress wields two lightsabers at once!

THIS DOES NOT SEEM VERY SAFE!

You decide to consult with Yoda. As the Grand Jedi Master, he might know how to find the Sith Lord who sent Asajj Ventress.

TURN TO **56**

OR

You are worried about further attacks. You fly to Coruscant to warn Chancellor Palpatine about the growing power of the Sith.

TURN TO **54**

MECHANICAL MASTER

Not only is Anakin a brilliant pilot, he is a skilled engineer, too. His experiences of building and repairing podracers when he was younger taught him how to modify any ship, including this Delta-7 starfighter.

SQUEEZED BY STRIKERS

You convince a few rebel ships to set course for the surface of Scarif in the hope of helping the rebels on the planet. But when you break away from the main fleet, you find yourself trapped between the energy shield that surrounds Scarif and a squad of fast-moving Imperial TIE strikers!

DATA FILE

TWIN ION ENGINE/SK X1 EXPERIMENTAL AIR SUPERIORITY FIGHTER

» Top speed: 1,500 kph (932 mph)

» 6 laser cannons

» Proton bomb chute

SHAPED FOR SPEED

Faster and better armed than a standard TIE fighter, the TIE striker's streamlined wings and lightweight hull make it extra-fast in a planet's atmosphere.

SQUEEZED FROM SCARIF

Going it alone has made you an easy target, and the TIE strikers are on your tail! Your only hope is to outrun them, and you flee the battle hoping the rebel fleet can win without you...

>> GO BACK AND CHOOSE ANOTHER PATH!

You are sorry to say goodbye to your friends on the *Ghost*, but you don't want to risk getting caught by the Empire again! They offer to loan you their shuttle, the *Phantom II*, which docks aboard the *Ghost*. You jump at the chance and head out into the unknown. But before long, you find yourself going backward!

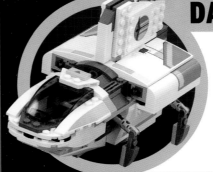

DATA FILE

PHANTOM II: MODIFIED *SHEATHIPEDE*-CLASS SHUTTLE

» Originally a Separatist ship in the Clone Wars

» 4 laser cannons

» Paintwork by rebel Sabine Wren

SECOND SHUTTLE

The *Phantom II* is a small ship that docks at the rear of the *Ghost*. The Spectres found it gathering dust and upgraded it after the first *Phantom* was destroyed during a dangerous mission.

CAUGHT IN THRAWN'S THRALL

Realizing you are caught in a tractor beam, you wish you had stayed on the stealthy *Ghost*! Your ship has been spotted by the Imperial mastermind Grand Admiral Thrawn—and now you are his prisoner!

>> GO BACK AND CHOOSE ANOTHER PATH

MAUL ON THE MOVE

Maul soars out of the palace hangar in his stealth ship, and you follow him in a Naboo starfighter. You ready your weapons as you near the upper atmosphere, but before you can fire a single shot, the Sith Lord engages his hyperdrive and disappears faster than lightspeed!

DATA FILE

SITH INFILTRATOR

» Also known as the *Scimitar*

» Top speed 1,180 kph (733 mph)

» 6 laser cannons

» Minelayer

SPIES IN THE SKY

Darth Maul's ship has a cloaking device that makes it almost impossible to detect. Aboard, he keeps a trio of DRK-1 probe droids that serve as flying spies on missions for his master, Darth Sidious.

Probe droids

SITH ESCAPE!

There is no way to track Maul's stealthy craft, so all you can do is return to Naboo. Queen Amidala is there when you land, and thanks you for foiling whatever Maul was planning. If only the despicable Sith hadn't gotten away!

>> GO BACK AND CHOOSE ANOTHER PATH!

When you get to the spaceport, you go looking in the local cantina for ways off Tatooine. Here, all sorts of characters can be found. In one corner, you spot a pair of likely smugglers, and in another you see a lone figure who might be a bounty hunter. They will definitely have ships, but who should you approach?

A HIVE OF VILLAINY

The Mos Eisley spaceport is a busy part of Tatooine. Stores and cantinas have grown up around its 362 starship landing bays, serving the many pilots, traders, fugitives, and career criminals who pass through every day.

Cantina barman

A BOTTLE OF YOUR FINEST OIL, PLEASE.

Choose the lone figure. Introduce yourself and inquire about a ride.

TURN TO 93

OR

Choose the smugglers. Say hello and ask to see their ship.

TURN TO 83

BUILD IT!

Make your own Mos Eisley spaceport, with landing bays, restaurants, market stalls, cargo transporters, security checkpoints, and more.

BATTLE REPORT

You climb into Gree's turbo tank, which has ten huge wheels for rolling over difficult terrain. Gree is using it as his operations base and gives a report: There is no Sith presence on Kashyyyk, but there are still droid forces to be fought. You help to plan for the next battle. The situation is under control—for now. It is time to track down the Sith! Where do you go next?

DATA FILE

HAVW A6 JUGGERNAUT

» Heavy laser turret

» Repeating laser

» Projectile launchers

Commander Gree

TURBO CARGO

The turbo tank is one of the Galactic Republic's main troop deployment methods. It carries equipment too, such as AT-RTs (All Terrain Recon Transports).

AT-RT

IT'S TIME TO CONTINUE OUR MISSION.

You have been on a wild Sith chase! Maybe the Sith were on Geonosis all along? Travel there before it's too late.

TURN TO **99**

OR

You establish contact with Jedi Anakin Skywalker, who says he can help you. Head into space to meet Anakin.

TURN TO **73**

When you join the Jedha street battle, it inspires Chirrut and Baze to fight twice as hard. Together, you blow up the Imperial tank. This attracts the attention of other rebels but also the Empire —who wants to rid the galaxy of rebel uprisings, and all of Jedha! You meet a Y-wing pilot who offers you a way out. Which of his options will you choose?

DATA FILE

BTL-A4 Y-WING ASSAULT STARFIGHTER/BOMBER

» Top speed 1,000 kph (621 mph)

» 2 laser cannons

» 2 ion cannons

SAVED FROM SCRAP

Y-wing fighters have been around since the days of the Clone Wars. The rebels stole the old ships from Imperial scrapyards and now work hard to keep them in shape for the fight against the Empire.

Follow the Y-wing pilot as far as the top-secret rebel base, where you can meet new allies.

TURN TO **14**

OR

The Y-wing pilot is heading into battle over the planet Scarif, where rebels desperately need more help. Go there.

TURN TO **107**

You throw yourself off the end of the plank and land on a skiff. What a narrow escape! Several of these small floating platforms surround Jabba's barge to defend it from attack. This one happens to be briefly unattended so you grab the controls and race away with U-3PO. Where will you go now?

DATA FILE

BANTHA-II CARGO SKIFF
- » Top speed 250 kph (155 mph)
- » Repulsorlift engine
- » Armor plating

SANDPROOF SHIP

Skiffs are well suited to the harsh conditions on Tatooine, with few complex parts that can be damaged by sandstorms. They are designed to carry cargo, but Jabba loads his with heavily armed guards.

> HOW ABOUT SOME DESSERT AND NO MORE DESERTS?

Stop at the first sign of civilization—the Mos Eisley cantina—to plot a way to get your own back on Jabba!

TURN TO **110**

OR

Head for the Mos Eisley spaceport to find a way off Tatooine and away from Jabba once and for all!

TURN TO **88**

BUILD IT!

Use different angles of slope brick to make realistic-looking sand dunes. Remember, sand can be any color on other planets!

A SECRET LAB

Following Anakin has led you here: the Grand Republic Medical Facility on Coruscant, the city planet. In this secret room, the powerful Sith Lord Darth Vader is being transformed into a terrifying man-machine! You should not have risked following Anakin. He has turned to the dark side and *he* is the Sith Lord Darth Vader!

TRANSFORMATION CHAMBER

Anakin was lured to the dark side by Darth Sidious, the leader of the Sith. Sidious oversees Anakin's mechanical transformation into a merciless cyborg monster.

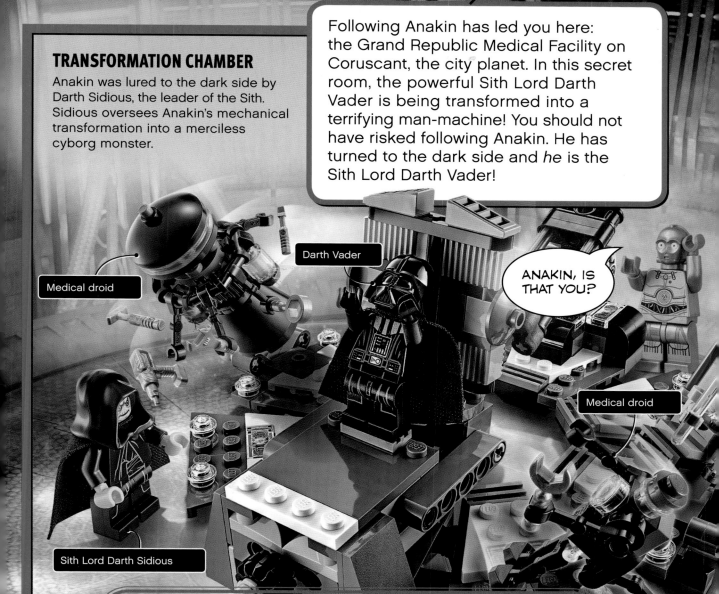

Medical droid

Darth Vader

ANAKIN, IS THAT YOU?

Medical droid

Sith Lord Darth Sidious

ARISE, LORD VADER!

Anakin tricked you. You should have listened to Obi-Wan. Anakin has become Darth Vader and he is now more dangerous than ever before!

>> GO BACK AND CHOOSE ANOTHER PATH!

GREETING GREEDO

You were right! The shady-looking character you spotted in the Mos Eisley cantina is a bounty hunter. He introduces himself as Greedo, and you tell him how you got there. He says can help you get off Tatooine —for a price. But you want to see his ship before making any deals…

SHARP SENSES

Greedo is a reptilian bounty hunter from the swamp planet Rodia. His large eyes see colors that humans do not, and his antennae can detect the slightest movement. He is willing to track down anyone for money!

BUILD IT!

Build a bounty hunter's spaceship for Greedo. Give it a prison cell and maybe a secret escape hatch that even Greedo doesn't know about!

ONE FOR THE RODIAN

As soon as you are inside his ship, Greedo pulls a blaster on you. He says the Empire is looking for escapees from the rebel ship *Tantive IV*, and it is sure to pay a good price for you!

>> GO BACK AND CHOOSE ANOTHER PATH!

SNOW SPEEDING

Your snowspeeder is one of several blasting out of Echo Base as the Empire attacks. The rebel forces are coordinating a fight back against the Imperial ground forces on Hoth's vast snowy plains. This will give the other rebels time to evacuate the base and escape. Should you help, or get away while you can?

DATA FILE

T-47 AIRSPEEDER
» Modified for use as snowspeeders
» Top speed 1,100 kph (684 mph)
» 2 laser cannons
» Harpoon and tow cable

ICE WARRIORS

Snowspeeders are attack craft that have been adapted for use in icy conditions. They have insulated side panels to protect their engines from extreme cold, and space for a rear gunner who can also deploy a tow cable.

Join the other snowspeeders in the Battle of Hoth as they take on a huge Imperial AT-AT walker. They need help!

TURN TO
106

OR

There's no time to stop! Echo Base is past saving. Race away to safety in your snowspeeder.

TURN TO
117

CALL THE COPS!

Hooray! You spot a police gunship as you enter Coruscant's lower atmosphere. You send it a message about the vulture droids. A reply comes through saying that the ship will escort you to a landing area, where you can make a full report to the onboard Coruscant Security Force officers.

DATA FILE

POLICE GUNSHIP
- » 3 laser cannons
- » Troop transport bay
- » Missile launchers
- » Searchlights
- » Solar panels for power

Shock trooper

YOU CAN'T ARREST ME! I'M LEAVING!

SPEEDY SHIP

The Coruscant Security Force (CSF) uses small gunships to chase crooks and respond to danger quickly in the densely packed city.

SHOCK! TROOPERS!

On the ground, you see that the gunship is full of fearsome elite shock troopers, not the Security Force police officers who you thought were going to help you! As the shock troopers surround you and take you prisoner, you realize that someone very powerful has led you into a trap!

» GO BACK AND CHOOSE ANOTHER PATH!

THE FINAL BATTLE

After weeks of training, Luke feels ready to face the galaxy's greatest villains —and you feel kind of like a Jedi, too! Together, you confront the evil Emperor in his throne room on the Death Star —but his right-hand man, the Dark Lord Vader, comes to his master's defense. The Emperor taunts you, challenging you to destroy Darth Vader—if you can!

SNEAKY SIDIOUS

The Emperor is really Darth Sidious, an evil Sith Lord who tricked the whole galaxy into thinking he was a wise and kindly ruler. He slowly took control of the galaxy before declaring it to be his Empire!

TELL ME WHEN IT'S ALL OVER!

END OF EMPIRE

You and Luke have the power to destroy Darth Vader, but together you choose not to. Your example causes Vader have a change of heart, and using the power of the Force he casts the Emperor into oblivion! The galaxy is free at last. You and Luke are heroes!

» GO BACK AND CHOOSE ANOTHER PATH!

GIVE UP THE *GHOST*?

As the *Ghost* takes off with you and U-3PO aboard, its captain, Hera Syndulla, picks up a message calling on all rebels to come to the planet Scarif. The rebels have usually worked in small clusters, but this is the first time they have been called to work together in an alliance. It could be a trap, so Hera gives you a choice: Will you stay or will you go?

DATA FILE

THE *GHOST*: MODIFIED VCX-100 LIGHT FREIGHTER

» Top speed 1,025 kph

» 3 laser cannons

» 2 proton torpedo launchers

GHOST WITH THE MOST

Hera called her ship the *Ghost* because it can vanish from Imperial sensors as if it were never there! Because its stealth systems are sometimes not enough, the vessel is also protected by two rotating gunner's stations.

Hera

Stay aboard the *Ghost* as it sets course for Scarif. The message sounded important.

TURN TO **107**

OR

Climb into the *Ghost's* onboard shuttle, *Phantom II*, in search of a new adventure.

TURN TO **86**

BUILD IT!

Rebel ships come in all shapes and sizes, and are often hastily patched up. Use unusual bricks to make the strangest rebel ship you can.

QUEEN OF THE CASTLE

The Force sensitive "pirate queen" Maz Kanata is more than 1,000 years old. Her castle home on Takodana was a peaceful hiding place for smugglers and renegades until a First Order attack left it in ruins.

Your Resistance friends bring you to the planet Takodana, where you meet the mysterious Maz Kanata. Many interesting people travel through Takodana and many choose to stay. You could safely hide here from the First Order! Maz senses the power of the Force is strong in Rey and she says that you were destined to come here...

LET'S TAK-O BREAK ON TAKODANA!

Maz

CAN YOU FEEL THE FORCE?

Maz says you can stay on Takodana until you have found a way to defeat the First Order. She thinks the Force is strong with you, so she knows you can do it! However, first you'll have to develop your abilities and start looking for allies who can help the Resistance. That's going to take some time!

>> GO BACK AND CHOOSE ANOTHER PATH!

GEONOSIS AMBUSH

Phew! Geonosis is HOT! This harsh planet is home to the insectoid Geonosians, but this part of the desert is empty. Suddenly, from nowhere, you come under attack from a Hailfire droid and a pair of B2 super battle droids! What do you do?

Missile launchers

I THINK IT IS TIME TO CALL FOR HELP. HELP!

ENEMY EYE

The *Hailfire*-class droid tank rolls into action on two huge wheels. It is a thinking machine rather than a vehicle, targeting its prey from great distances with one unblinking red eye.

FORCE FACT!

Super battle droids are far more powerful than basic battle droids. They have heavy armor and built-in blasters, and do not rely on orders from a control ship.

You need backup! You contact local clone troops—luckily there is a tank nearby.

TURN TO **111**

OR

You don't think ground troops will be enough. You order an airstrike, but will the clones arrive in time?

TURN TO **39**

BUILD IT!

Try building a vehicle with one major feature as a starting point, such as a huge wheel, a laser cannon, or a special eye (like the Hailfire droid tank).

THE JAWS OF DOOM

You look down into the pit and see the dangerous monster that lives inside: a huge, gaping mouth surrounded by tentacles. This is the Sarlacc—one of Jabba's many petrifying pets—and most of it is under the ground! When you don't jump, one of Jabba's thugs pushes both you and U-3PO in!

BURIED BEAST

Sarlaccs are related to other scary species such as the rathtar. Their huge, buried bodies include several stomachs for digesting prey, and they can live for tens of thousands of years!

SNACK FOR A SARLACC

As you plummet toward the Sarlacc's mouth, you realize that your adventure is almost certainly over. You can only hope that U-3PO's metal body will be enough to make the monster spit you both back out!

>> GO BACK AND CHOOSE ANOTHER PATH!

On the desert planet Seelos you meet with Captain Rex. A brave Republic trooper during the Clone Wars, Rex now lives with his fellow old soldiers Gregor and Wolffe in a customized AT-TE. Your mission here with Phoenix Squadron is to help him defend his home from an Imperial attack!

DATA FILE

MODIFIED ALL TERRAIN TACTICAL ENFORCER

» Heavily modified to make a home

» Mass driver cannon still functions

» Adapted for catching giant Joopa worms

Captain Rex

Commander Wolffe

Commander Gregor

Imperial Inquisitor Fifth Brother

MOBILE HOME

Captain Rex's AT-TE is a battle walker built to fight in the Clone Wars. When the wars ended, Rex set about turning it into a home, with little luxuries such as beds and a kitchen!

STAY ON SEELOS

Fighting alongside the old clone troopers, you realize that this is going to be a long battle. If you stay here you might be on Seelos for some time! There is plenty of space aboard Rex's AT-TE, but you wonder if you could have helped more by answering that distress call...

>> GO BACK AND CHOOSE ANOTHER PATH!

In the swamps of Dagobah, a planet in a faraway corner of the galaxy, you meet Yoda—a small but powerful Jedi Master. Yoda says Luke was drawn there by his connection to the Force, and if he stays, he can learn to be a great Jedi. But Luke wants to use his Force powers now to take on the Empire. What can you do to help?

> WISE MASTER YODA IS, BUT TALK FUNNY, HE DOES.

EXILED BY EMPIRE

Yoda went to live on Dagobah when the Empire took over the galaxy. He built himself a simple hut, where he spends his days alone, learning all he can about the mysteries of the Force.

You want Luke to become a powerful Jedi. Convince him to stay with Yoda and train to use his Force powers.

TURN TO **96**

OR

Leave with Luke so the pair of you can challenge the Empire right away. Taking on the dark side can't wait!

TURN TO **109**

GLORY TO THE GUNGANS!

You leave the underwater city with the Gungan Army and head for Naboo's Great Grass Plains to face the advancing battle droids. With your encouragement, the Gungans overwhelm the droids and their Armored Assault Tanks, and win the Battle of Naboo. You leave the battlefield a hero and Naboo can become a peaceful planet again—but you still have a Sith Lord to find! Where could he be?

DATA FILE

ARMORED ASSAULT TANK (AAT)

» Top speed 55 kph (34 mph)

» 4 lateral lasers

» Energy shell launchers

» Also available in blue!

TRADE WARRIORS

Armored Assault Tanks are hovering vehicles used by the droid armies of the greedy Trade Federation and the Separatists. Small but heavily armed, they can glide over most terrain, blasting everything that gets in their way.

Some guards have heard a disturbance back at Naboo's Theed Palace. There is a rumor that this is sinister Sith activity. Race there at once!

TURN TO 51

OR

You don't believe the rumor. Queen Amidala no longer needs you on Naboo so you decide to leave and head to Coruscant. Perhaps the Sith are there!

TURN TO 30

THESE DROIDS MUST HAVE AN "OFF" SWITCH!

You were right not to follow the footprints! You soon find Luke, but he is injured and has been out in the cold too long. To recover, he needs to spend some time in a bacta tank. However, while Luke is in the tank, the base comes under Imperial attack! You need to get Luke to safety, but how?

MEDICATED GOO

Bacta is a thick fluid that helps people's injuries to heal faster. If someone has been badly hurt, they can be placed inside a whole tank of bacta. It's gloopy, but it's good for you!

IMPERIALS ARE FOLLOWING US EVERYWHERE!

Rebel protocol droid R-3PO

Medical droid

Luke in bacta tank

Pluck Luke from the tank and ride away with him on a tauntaun, a creature often used by the rebels.

TURN TO **68**

OR

Fly the injured Luke away from the base in a snowspeeder—a vehicle modified especially for snow.

TURN TO **94**

BUILD IT!

Use slopes and curved pieces to build a part of Echo Base that is melting from the heat of the Empire's attack.

You know that the Sith Lord Count Dooku is nearby but you struggle to locate his sleek ship, the Solar Sailer. The yacht can travel without using its engines, which makes it *very* hard to detect. You race ahead and finally have the Sith Lord's ship in your sight… until Dooku spots you and picks up speed!

DATA FILE

PUNWORCCA **116-CLASS INTERSTELLAR SLOOP**

» Top speed 1,600 kph (1,000 mph)

» 84 narrow-beam tractor/repulsor emitters

INFINITE FUEL

Dooku's ship is made from precious Geonosian metals. Its wings open like a flower to capture streams of interstellar energy, which provides an endless source of fuel.

DODGED BY DOOKU

You try to catch up with the Solar Sailer, but Dooku's ship is far quicker than your own, and anyway, you don't want to risk getting caught in its tractor beams! As Dooku speeds off, you wish you had faced him on the ground instead!

>> GO BACK AND CHOOSE ANOTHER PATH!

As you race into battle, you see that Luke is feeling better. He suggests using the snowspeeder's tow line to trip up an approaching AT-AT, and this trick brings the AT-AT crashing to the ground! As the other snowspeeders follow your example, Luke experiences a sudden strange feeling. What could it mean?

DATA FILE

ALL TERRAIN ARMORED TRANSPORT

» Top speed 60 kph (37 mph)

» 2 heavy blaster cannons

» 2 medium blasters

WALKING WEAPONS

AT-ATs (All Terrain Armored Transports) are four-legged combat walkers used by the Empire. At a distance, they look like enormous animals, but up close they are clearly tanks, with huge blaster cannons mounted on their "heads."

Luke feels like he must fly to a place called Dagobah, so you take him there.

TURN TO
102

OR

You think Luke needs to defeat the Empire, so you take him directly to the Emperor!

TURN TO
112

When you reach Scarif, you see hundreds of rebel ships battling a huge Imperial fleet in orbit. A U-wing fighter sends you a message to say there is a rebel strike force on a vital mission on the planet below, trying to steal the plans to the Empire's new Death Star superweapon. The Empire must not be allowed to stop them! How can you help?

DATA FILE

UT-60D U-WING STARFIGHTER

» Top speed 950 kph (590 mph)

» 2 laser cannons

» 2 ion blasters

» Space for 8 passengers

U-TURN

The U-wing is an able starfighter, but its main purpose is to deliver troops into battle on the ground. In combat, it turns its wings backward to extend the range of its deflector field.

Add the firepower of your ship to the rebels repelling the Empire's ships in orbit above Scarif.

TURN TO **116**

OR

Break away from the battle and try to help the team down on the planet's surface.

TURN TO **85**

Aboard the Resistance transporter, you take off after the stormtroopers on their speeder. You are about to target weapons on the small craft's engines when a First Order shuttle swoops out of hyperspace! You fire at the newcomer, but it has no effect. It is Kylo Ren's own sinister-looking command shuttle, and it is very heavily armed and shielded!

DATA FILE

UPSILON-CLASS COMMAND SHUTTLE

» 2 heavy laser cannons

» Folding durasteel wings

» Sensor-jamming stealth technology

FAMILY HISTORY

Kylo Ren is the son of rebel heroes Han Solo and Leia Organa. He trained to be a Jedi, but became fascinated by his late grandfather, Sith Lord Darth Vader. Now he serves the First Order!

ROUTED BY REN

The speeder must have called for help—and the call has been answered by the First Order's most fearsome warrior of all! Kylo Ren easily overpowers your ship and comes to deal with you in person. Gulp!

>> GO BACK AND CHOOSE ANOTHER PATH!

NONE SHALL PASS!

Eager to free the galaxy from the harsh rule of the Empire, you leave Dagobah with Luke and head straight for the Emperor's throne room. You know that Luke is strong with the Force, and can't wait to see him wield his power. But when you arrive, your way is barred by the Emperor's imposing Royal Guard!

SEEING RED

The Royal Guard is an elite squad of soldiers responsible for protecting the Emperor. As a Sith Lord with vast Force powers, the Emperor doesn't actually need them, but their grand appearance appeals to his self-importance.

CAN'T WE USE THE FORCE TO GET OUT OF THIS SITUATION?

A ROYAL ARREST

Luke is powerful, but having refused Yoda's Jedi training, he is no match for the Emperor's strongest and most feared protectors—and neither are you! You don't even see the Emperor before the two of you are taken prisoner!

>> GO BACK AND CHOOSE ANOTHER PATH!

At the cantina, you come up with a plan while you listen to the musicians on stage. When they take a break, you ask if you can join their band. You have heard that they often play at Jabba's Palace, so it's the perfect way to get close to the horrid Hutt and pay him back for his cruelty!

BUILD IT!

Combine small elements to make unusual musical instruments for your minifigures. See if you can build a whole mini alien orchestra!

Figrin D'an and fellow Bith band member

THIS SOLO IS REALLY GOING SOMEWHERE!

INTRODUCING THE BAND

Figrin D'an and the Modal Nodes are a popular band on Tatooine. They specialize in up-tempo Bith jazz and smooth jatz. Originally from the planet Bith, they often play for the pilots, smugglers, and bounty hunters at the Mos Eisley cantina.

REVENGE WITH THE BITH

The band leader, Figrin D'an, says you can join —but only if you learn to play the kloo horn! As you sit down for the first of many lessons, you begin to wonder whether hiding out with the band or plotting revenge will be as fun as you first imagined!

>> GO BACK AND CHOOSE ANOTHER PATH!

DATA FILE

ALL TERRAIN TACTICAL ENFORCER
» Top speed
  160 kpm (99mph)
» 4 front laser cannons
» 2 rear laser cannons
» Mass-driver cannon

Help is coming! A six-legged tank storms toward you and blasts away the attacking battle droids. The All-Terrain Tactical Enforcer (AT-TE) may not be the fastest walker, but it is the most stable and is *very* heavily armed. You board the AT-TE and meet legendary Jedi Master Mace Windu.

VERSATILE WALKER

AT-TE's six articulated legs provide good grip, allowing the walker to climb steep slopes. Their magnetized feet can cling to larger craft in space.

I THOUGHT HELP WOULD NEVER ARRIVE!

FORCE FACT!
-- --- --
Mace Windu is one of the most respected members of the Jedi High Council and a fearsome warrior. He is the only Jedi to wield a purple lightsaber!

GROUNDED ON GEONOSIS

Your ships were destroyed by the attacking droids, so Mace Windu invites you and Obi-Wan to travel with him on the AT-TE. It is too slow for hunting a Sith Lord and cannot fly, so for now you must continue your fight against evil by battling droids on Geonosis!

»» GO BACK AND CHOOSE ANOTHER PATH!

DEATH STAR SHOCK!

You and Luke break away from the rebel fleet to confront Emperor Palpatine—the Sith Lord Darth Sidious. Luke senses great evil near the Forest Moon of Endor, so you set course and speed there through hyperspace. You arrive to see a terrible sight: a brand new Death Star battle station nearing completion!

DATA FILE

DEATH STAR II

» 30,000 turbolasers

» 1 superlaser

» Incomplete hull leaves some decks exposed

SECOND SPHERE

After its first Death Star was destroyed, the Empire began building one that was bigger and even more powerful. Most importantly, this replacement would not have the thermal exhaust port that was the first one's weak spot!

STRIKING TOO SOON

Luke was right: the Emperor is here! But his battle station is fully operational, and the two of you are no match for it—yet! As you flee its laser fire, you wish you had gone to Dagobah first...

>> GO BACK AND CHOOSE ANOTHER PATH!

EWOK ALLIANCE

You ask U-3PO to translate the Ewoks' excited chatter, and he says they dislike the Empire as much as you! Together, you head for the Imperial power station and join up with the rebels. Ewoks may look harmless, but they fight fiercely! They distract the guards as you sneak inside. You cut the power being sent to the Death Star, leaving the superweapon unshielded!

UNWANTED VISITORS

The Ewoks knew nothing of the Empire before it built its new Death Star over Endor's moon. When a ground station was built to provide power to the Death Star's shields, it shattered the peace on the Ewoks' forest world.

Ewok glider

Princess Leia

R2-D2

Han Solo

BUILD IT!

Make a complex-looking power generator by using lots of small parts as lights, levers, dials, cables, pipes, and vents!

POWER TO THE PEOPLE

A flash of light in the sky lets you know that the rebels have seized the chance you have given them and blown up the now-unshielded Death Star. Now you can celebrate the end of the Empire with the Ewoks. Hooray!

>> GO BACK AND CHOOSE ANOTHER PATH!

The bombers you are following are on a mission to defend the Resistance base on Crait from a First Order attack. When you arrive, you are shocked to find a far bigger enemy force than anyone had expected! Heavy scout walkers and First Order fighters are scuttling all over the planet's snowy surface. It's going to take some sharp shooting from the *Falcon* to stop them!

DATA FILE

HEAVY SCOUT WALKER

» Cockpit carries First Order officer and gunner

» Crawling legs hide wheels

» Side- and front-mounted blasters

CRAIT ESCAPES

Back when the Empire ruled the galaxy, the Rebel Alliance had a secret base on the planet Crait. With the rise of the First Order, it also became a hideout for the Resistance, but has now been invaded by First Order scout walkers, among other vehicles.

Resistance trooper

General Hux

RESISTANCE REWARD

With you at the laser cannon controls, the *Falcon* scythes through the scout walkers, shattering their spidery metal legs. Later, General Leia rewards you with a medal for your bravery!

>> GO BACK AND CHOOSE ANOTHER PATH!

BATTLE ON MUSTAFAR

Anakin brings you to Mustafar, a burning planet of lava, erupting volcanoes, and swirling ash that blocks the sun. You and Obi-Wan accuse Anakin of turning to the dark side. Anakin says he promised to take you to a Sith Lord—and he has!

THE RED PLANET

Droids mine the boiling landscape for valuable minerals and villains hide out in the scorched black mountains. Beneath the bubbling lava is a vast system of caves. The lava field is an unstable surface for a lightsaber battle.

Lava mining platform

MY COGS ARE MELTING. IT'S TIME TO LEAVE THIS PLANET!

VADER REVEALED!

Anakin reveals that he now goes by the name Darth Vader, and he is the Sith Lord you have been searching for! With your help, Obi-Wan battles Vader in fierce lightsaber combat and eventually wins the battle. Together you have saved the galaxy from evil. You're a hero!

>> GO BACK AND CHOOSE ANOTHER PATH!

Every little starship helps in the battle against the Empire! With your combined firepower, you hold the Empire at bay just long enough for the team down on Scarif to complete its mission. This brave band of rebels, led by Jyn Erso and assisted by Cassian Andor, has won a great victory. When you hear the job is done, it's time to hit the hyperdrive!

BUILD IT!

Build a landing platform for ships using flat gray tiles. Send shoretroopers flying by placing a hinge plate beneath a tile and creating a seesaw action!

Cassian Andor

Jyn Erso in Imperial disguise

Imperial shoretrooper

ROGUE ONE REBELS

Scarif looks tropical and idyllic, but hides an enormous Imperial base. Jyn Erso's team of rebels sneaks onto the surface in a stolen Imperial ship that has been renamed Rogue One.

MISSION ACCOMPLISHED

As you fly away from Scarif, you learn what the mission was all about. You have just helped to steal the secret plans of the Empire's greatest weapon—the Death Star! This could be the start of a brand new era. Well done!

>> GO BACK AND CHOOSE ANOTHER PATH!

REBEL RETREAT

The snowspeeders fly into battle, leaving you free to escape from the base. You and Luke board a huge rebel transport ship as the rebel fleet takes off from Hoth and abandons Echo Base for good. Getting the fleet away in one piece is a kind of victory. With Echo Base in ruins, where do you go next?

Imperial probe droid

ECHO CHAMBERS

The rebels hoped the Empire wouldn't find them on Hoth, but were prepared in case they did. Echo Base is big enough to hide the entire rebel fleet, with huge bay doors for a quick escape into space.

SNOW LONG, HOTH! TIME TO GET OUT OF HERE.

Imperial snowtrooper

Now that Luke is healed, you follow him to the planet Dagobah to learn about his Force powers.

TURN TO **102**

OR

Travel in the transport ship to the rebels' new base—a ship known as *Home One*.

TURN TO **5**

DUEL WITH DOOKU

Your pursuit of Count Dooku leads you to a hangar on Geonosis, where Dooku has landed his ship. Dooku was once a Jedi Master, but he has spent many years learning the power of the dark side. As you enter the hangar, you discover Dooku is battling Obi-Wan and Anakin! You and Yoda have arrived just in time. Head into the fray!

DUELING WITH DOOKU

Only a Sith would use a lightsaber with a red blade! Count Dooku's lightsaber has a curved hilt design, which allows him to use it with greater precision in lightsaber duels.

MASTER YODA DOESN'T NEED WINGS TO FLY!

DOOKU DEFEATED

It takes all of Yoda's strength, but with your help he saves Obi-Wan's and Anakin's lives. Good job! Unfortunately, as you and Yoda rush to your Jedi friends, Count Dooku manages to flee. But now exposed as a Sith Lord, Dooku can no longer move freely through the galaxy —he is forced into a life of fear and hiding.

>> GO BACK AND CHOOSE ANOTHER PATH!

GLOSSARY

UNDERSTANDING THESE WORDS WILL HELP YOU TO MAKE GOOD CHOICES THROUGHOUT THE BOOK!

BOUNTY HUNTER
Someone who is paid to find or destroy people or objects.

CHANCELLOR
The leader of the Republic.

CLONE
An identical copy of a living thing, created in a lab.

CLONE WARS
A series of galaxy-wide battles between the Republic's Clone Army and the Separatists' Droid Army.

DEATH STAR
A huge Imperial battle station, with enough firepower to destroy an entire planet.

DROID
A robot who can be programed to work for a certain purpose—or person.

EMPEROR
The ruler of the Empire.

EMPIRE
A cruel government that rules the galaxy under the leadership of Emperor Palpatine, a Sith Lord.

FIRST ORDER
A powerful organization created from the remains of the Empire. Its aim is to take control of the galaxy.

THE FORCE
The energy that flows through all living things. It can be used for good or evil.

HYPERDRIVE
Part of a starship that allows it to travel faster than the speed of light.

HYPERSPACE
An extra dimension of space, used by experienced starship pilots to travel faster than lightspeed.

IMPERIAL ARMY

The Empire's huge army, which includes stormtroopers.

JEDI

A member of the Jedi Order who studies the light side of the Force.

JEDI ORDER

An ancient group of Force users that promotes peace and justice throughout the galaxy.

KYBER CRYSTAL

A precious type of crystal that channels the Force to power a lightsaber.

LIGHTSABER

A sword-like weapon with a blade of pure energy that is used by Jedi and Sith.

LIGHTSPEED

A special kind of travel that allows a spaceship to cross vast distances in an instant.

PADAWAN

A Jedi apprentice who is training to become a fully-fledged Jedi Knight.

REBEL ALLIANCE

The group that resists and fights the Empire.

REPUBLIC

The democratic government that rules many planets in the galaxy.

RESISTANCE

The group that defends the galaxy from the First Order.

SEPARATISTS

A group that is opposed to the Republic and tries to break away from it.

SITH

An ancient group of Force users who seek to use the dark side of the Force to gain power.

TRADE FEDERATION

A bureaucratic organization that controls much of the trade and commerce in the galaxy.

DK | Penguin Random House

Senior Editors Emma Grange, Helen Murray
Senior Designer Anna Formanek
Project Art Editor Rhys Thomas
Designer Gema Salamanca
Editorial Assistant Joseph Stewart
Senior Pre-Production Producer Jennifer Murray
Producer Lloyd Robertson
Managing Editor Paula Regan
Managing Art Editor Jo Connor
Art Director Lisa Lanzarini
Publisher Julie Ferris
Publishing Director Simon Beecroft

First American Edition, 2018
Published in the United States by DK Publishing
345 Hudson Street, New York, New York 10014

Page design copyright © 2018 Dorling Kindersley
Limited
DK, a Division of Penguin Random House LLC
18 19 20 21 22 10 9 8 7 6 5 4 3 2
003–307586–June/18

For Lucasfilm:
Executive Editor Jennifer Heddle
Art Director Troy Alders
Story Group Leland Chee, Pablo Hidalgo, Matt Martin,
Rayne Roberts, and James Waugh

DK would like to thank: Randi Sørensen, Heidi K. Jensen,
Paul Hansford, and Martin Leighton Lindhardt at the
LEGO Group; Julia March for proofreading; Hannah
Gulliver-Jones and Shari Last for editorial assistance,
and Lisa Sodeau for design assistance.

First published in Great Britain in 2018 by
Dorling Kindersley Limited
80 Strand, London, WC2R 0RL
A Penguin Random House Company

Page design copyright © 2018 Dorling Kindersley Limited

A catalog record for this book is available from the
Library of Congress.

ISBN 978-1-4654-6756-0
ISBN 978-1-4654-7452-0 (library edition)

DK books are available at special discounts when
purchased in bulk for sales promotions, premiums,
fund-raising, or educational use.
For details, contact: DK Publishing Special
Markets, 345 Hudson Street, New York, New York 10014
SpecialSales@dk.com

Printed and bound in China.

A WORLD OF IDEAS:
SEE ALL THERE IS TO KNOW

www.dk.com

www.starwars.com

www.LEGO.com